Praise for
Wendy Isnardi

"*I will never forget my first meeting with Wendy. She appeared in my office with her husband holding her newborn daughter, and also accompanied by her mother. She was trembling, extremely anxious and sad. She was frightened of her own thoughts and fearful that she would do something wrong and that she could cause harm to her baby. Wendy was depressed and had obsessive thinking. She could not grasp what was going on with her. Yet, she expressed an inner desire to be the mother she always wanted to be. With professional help, the support of her family and medication, she was able to slowly grow to become more receptive to treatment, which included cognitive-behavioral therapy and exposure and response prevention. Slowly Wendy began to face her fears, taking small steps, tolerating her anxiety and beginning to enjoy motherhood. And now—look at her!! A loving, caring and educated mother of two beautiful daughters who is sharing her experience to help enlighten mothers going through difficult times during and after pregnancy. I applaud Wendy for all she has accomplished. It has been my privilege to walk along beside her at one time as her therapist. Now she walks on her own with confidence and pride.*"

—Irene Margolis, LCSW-RN

"*Wendy has written a very poignant book regarding her personal battle with postpartum depression.* Nobody Told Me *describes Wendy's own experience with postpartum depression in a very intimate and sensitive way. I highly recommend this compelling book to pregnant mothers and all mothers who have or may experience postpartum depression.*"

—Lori Green, RN BS FACCE
Lamaze Certified Childbirth Educator

Praise for
Wendy Isnardi

"In a candid style and with an open heart, Wendy Isnardi invites the reader into the intimate details of her experience with postpartum depression. Enveloped by relentless destructive images and horrifying thoughts, she shares the terror and emotional chaos as she struggled to discover what was happening to her. Nobody Told Me will make you pay attention to the critical importance of risk assessment, and prevention as an essential part of regular prenatal care."

—Diana Lynn Barnes, Psy.D., MFT
The Center for Postpartum Health

"Nobody told me either! I hope more and more mothers will add their voices, like Wendy, to the growing chorus of moms who say 'nobody told me,' until we become so loud that the world will wake up and start doing all that is necessary to educate and help new mothers."

—Katherine Stone, Postpartum Progress
http://www.postpartumprogress.com

"Isnardi's emotional journey after the birth of her baby is an honest and intimate account of the anguish that can accompany postpartum obsessive-compulsive disorder. Nobody Told Me bravely challenges the stigma of this agonizing illness while simultaneously offering comfort and hope to those who suffer."

—Karen Kleiman, MSW
Founder and Director
The Postpartum Stress Center, LLC
1062 Lancaster Ave, Suite 2
Rosemont, Pennsylvania 19010

Nobody Told Me

Nobody Told Me

My Battle with Postpartum Depression & Obsessive-Compulsive Disorder

Wendy Isnardi

Legwork Team Publishing
New York

Legwork Team Publishing
80 Davids Drive, Suite One
Hauppauge, NY 11788
www.legworkteam.com
Phone: 631-944-6511

ISBN: 978-1-935905-04-2 (sc)
ISBN: 978-1-935905-05-9 (hc)

First edition 01/14/2011

Printed in the United States of America
This book is printed on acid-free paper

Cover design and photography by
Tommy B.A. Cuevas
727-517-5561
theamazingtommy@gmail.com
http://darkmindofjello.deviantart.com/

I dedicate this to my beautiful daughters
Madison and Evangeline, my mother,
and the love of my life, my husband Joey.

Grandpa, I know you are watching over me.
"Sing, Sing, Sing."

"When you are a mother, you are never
really alone in your thoughts.
A mother always has to think twice,
once for herself
and once for her child."

—Sophia Loren

Contents

Contents

Foreword by
Sonia Murdock

*W*endy Isnardi is someone who cares enough to tell it like it is. I got to know Wendy well after she recovered from a perinatal mood and anxiety disorder, including obsessive-compulsive disorder. She completed several of our Volunteer Trainings and has served in many volunteer capacities as *a Mom on Call* Telephone Support Volunteer, Resource Coordinator, *Circle of Caring* Support Group Peer Facilitator, a Family Night Speaker, and a Public Speaker.

Wendy's goal from the very beginning has been to offer hope to help others. Now in *Nobody Told Me: My Battle with Postpartum Depression and Obsessive-Compulsive Disorder*, she provides a unique "insider's view" from her motherhood experience. She tells her story with candor and a passion that will help break through the stigma of such a currently misunderstood and taboo illness. Reading Wendy's book will be invaluable for women, families and anyone working with pregnant and postpartum women to further gain an understanding of this devastating illness.

As co-founder of the Postpartum Resource Center of New York and a past president of Postpartum Support International (PSI), I am grateful to Wendy for her hard work and commitment to help support mothers and families suffering from a perinatal mood and anxiety disorder.

Thank you, Wendy and also to your husband Joey and your mom

Pat, who I call the *Dream Team*. Your courage to speak out is an inspiration to women and families now and for future generations.

Sonia Murdock
Executive Director and Co-founder
Postpartum Resource Center of New York, Inc.
www.postpartumny.org

Preface

The decision to write this book was not an easy one. My experience with postpartum depression and obsessive-compulsive disorder completely changed me into the person I am today. Postpartum depression (PPD) is a general term used to describe a wide range of emotional disorders a woman can experience after the birth of her child. Three types of disorders are generally recognized: The baby blues, postpartum depression, and postpartum psychosis. Obsessive-Compulsive Disorder (OCD) is disorder of the brain and behavior. OCD causes severe anxiety in those affected. OCD involves both obsessions and compulsions that take a lot of time and get in the way of important activities the person values. The two combined together form postpartum obsessive-compulsive disorder. The title *Nobody Told Me* means exactly what it implies; postpartum depression (PPD) is real, and the subject was never broached before, during or after my pregnancy. Nobody ever told me about the harrowing journey I was about to face. I wrote this book in order to help every woman and family member who has the misfortune of spiraling into depression after the birth of a child—a wonderful and anticipated event that we seem to take for granted. If this book can reach just one person and let her know she is not alone and there is help for her, perhaps a tragedy can be diverted and a beautiful life can be saved. They say every cloud has a silver lining, but with every precious gem stowed upon this earth, we must all dig through a little dirt to find it. I open my life to you; take this trip with me into a dark place filled with sadness, anxiety and horrible depression so that you too can see that a light can emerge from the dark. With some much-needed help and love, perhaps every woman who bears a child can say, "Somebody told me."

Introduction

*O*n, July 15, 2002, my life changed forever. At first, it was for the best, then for the worst, and back again to the best that it ever gets. The birth of my daughter Madison was and is one of the greatest joys of my life. I woke up that morning with the worst cramps I have ever experienced. The next thing I knew I was having an emergency C-section, which wasn't what I expected, and had to stay in the hospital for a week. In that time, I learned how to feed, change, bathe and care for my newborn child. The nurses prepared my husband and me for the new journey that was ahead of us, telling us what to expect in the weeks to come. In that week not once did anyone, doctors or nurses, mention the possibility of postpartum depression, not even the baby blues. Not one person mentioned the risk of what could change my life and impair my ability to care for my child or myself.

I was sent home with a folder bulging with information on my newborn. From soup to nuts, it was packed with information about the baby, but not one piece of paper to prepare me for the possibility of what could happen. The day I stepped foot into my house with my newborn bundle of joy, I was a bundle of nerves! Never did I expect the nightmare that my life would become in the weeks that followed. For the first time, I truly wanted to die, and I didn't understand why.

Why me? Why did this happen? Why was I having horrible,

torturous thoughts and devastating anxiety? But most of all, why did the overwhelming feelings of love and attachment to my beautiful newborn baby get taken away from me? Was there a reason why? I was about to find out all by myself because nobody told me . . .

Wendy 101

I guess I should start from the beginning. My life was very normal: sadly, nothing extraordinarily different from many other families. I was born in Brooklyn, New York in the '70s to Patricia and a man I will call the sperm donor. My mother was a very young bride in the '60s, giving birth to my brother Michael shortly after her wedding. A few years after that, I was born. Everything seemed normal on the outside, but soon after my birth, things started falling apart. The sperm donor dabbled in show business, landing a few roles as an extra in some films. My mother's dream was to be a stay-at-home mother, but she had to get a job because the sperm donor was "laid off" from his. That seemed to be his M.O.—either getting "laid off" or fired, never really keeping down a job for longer than a few months. His love was stunt work, and even after I was born; he was still trying

1

to pursue a career in movies. He went so far as to have portfolios made up for my brother Michael and me, getting us auditions for commercials and extras in movies. We had some success making commercials and print ads, but nothing crazy. Neither my brother nor I had any interest in any of it. We were being pushed by the sperm donor to carry on. I was becoming belligerent at the auditions, defying whatever the producers would ask of me. Finally my mother just put an end to it because she knew how much I despised it. I just wanted to be a kid!

My father was a dreamer, always looking to get rich quick, but never succeeding. In three short years, we had moved in and out of several apartments. We even lived with my grandparents. Finally, the sperm donor got a steady job making good money, and we started living in a very exclusive apartment building in Brooklyn, doorman and all.

My parents started fighting a lot, and my mom was crying all the time. The sperm donor quit his job and opened an automobile repair shop a few hours away from our house. The sperm donor wasn't coming home for days on end, always with some crazy excuse. My mother had enrolled me in nursery school because she was working all the way in Manhattan, and the sperm donor was so unreliable that she needed to know that I was in a safe place with responsible adults. My brother was already in elementary school and was spending his days with my grandparents until my mother got home from work.

I remember being awoken one night to the sound of dishes breaking in the kitchen. My mother was screaming on the phone and having some kind of mental breakdown. Apparently the sperm donor was spending his days and nights with another woman. This "other woman" decided to call my mother in the middle of the night to tell her that the sperm donor was living with her and wouldn't be coming home again. He lived like this for a few months until this "other woman" threw him out, and my mother graciously took him back.

In an effort to save their marriage, my parents decided to move the family to a horse farm upstate in White Sulfer Springs, New York. Michael and I went into culture shock. Our house was on 36 acres of land, which meant our next-door neighbor was miles away. We had to walk to a general store to get our mail. The entire school, K-12, was in one building. My circle of friends consisted of my brother Michael, horses, some snakes, salamanders and my imagination. Talk about boring! Both parents found jobs in their fields, but my father was soon fired because he was caught messing around with the boss's daughter. Once again, my mother forgave him. The sperm donor, being the dreamer, decided to start a camp of sorts for stuntmen, teaching stunts! We had so much property that he figured he would use it to his benefit. To no one's surprise, that failed too! And with that, he found himself with some spare time and a new girlfriend. After two years of country living, we were packing it up and moving back to Brooklyn.

My parents separated briefly but got back together. My mom, Michael and I were living with my grandmother until my parents found a new place for us to live. They found a house on Long Island, and we were on our way to suburban living. I guess you can say this was the beginning of the end for my parents. My mother got herself another job working in Manhattan, and the sperm donor found a job working at a local car dealership as a mechanic. No more show business for him. Things were normal for a while; we were a family again. So it is said, old habits die hard; before we knew it, the sperm donor started disappearing again. He would go hunting on a Friday and not return for months. He would go to get milk and not return for days. On the rare occasion that he would come home, he always had boxes and boxes of fresh baked pies. Evidently his new girlfriend owned a pie stand and had no conscience, so he would bring the pies home to his family. He would deny his infidelity, telling my mother that he was living with friends and needed to get his head together.

The sperm donor made one last appearance as my mother's husband before she ultimately filed for legal separation in 1981, after sixteen years of torture. My parents stayed together until I was nine. Leaving the sperm donor was the smartest decision my mother ever made. The sperm donor, being the humanitarian, felt he hadn't tortured my mother enough, mentally. My mother was hospitalized due to severe back injury, although I think it was a nervous breakdown. While she was in the hospital, Michael and I stayed with the sperm donor at our home. It was supposed to last only until my mother got out of the hospital, but the sperm donor had a different plan. He was going to move us out of our house and into a new house—the home of his new fiancée. Long story short, when my mother was finally released from the hospital, she came home to find that house had gone into foreclosure, and her children were gone. The sperm donor had even gone as far as enrolling us in a new school district. If it hadn't been for my grandparents and aunt, I don't know if my mother would still be here. They kept her going and gave her the strength she needed to carry on.

My mother has always been my hero. She took that devastating and horrible circumstance and completely turned around her life, truly coming out on top. She stayed with her parents in Brooklyn during the week and saw Michael and me on the weekends. Around that time, she started dating a family friend, Vito. He helped her pick up all the pieces in her life. While working in Manhattan, she was going to school at night to finish her degree, and she became an insurance investigator. In the meantime, the sperm donor got married and impregnated his new wife right after my parents' divorce was finalized. My mother found herself an excellent lawyer and gained custody of me. Michael, on the other hand, was sixteen and able to make his own decision; he stayed with the sperm donor because he didn't want to change schools once again. My mother and Vito got engaged and bought a house. For the first time, my mother and I had the stability and truth in our lives that we truly deserved. In October of 1983, my mother and Vito got married.

The sperm donor and his second wife gave birth to my brother, Tommy, in 1984. I was happy to have a new little baby brother and hoped that the sperm donor wouldn't screw up his life, too. About a year after Tommy was born, the sperm donor was moving out; he found greener pastures. But that also meant Michael was out. Michael moved in with my mom and Vito. He finished his senior year in a new school district and finally found himself some stability, too. Eventually, the sperm donor's second wife took him back, only to get divorced years later. Getting married, divorced and ruining peoples lives would become the blueprint of the sperm donor's life. I call him a professional gigolo because he is very good and gets paid very well to do these things. I learned a lot from the sperm donor, most importantly not to be like him. When I was younger, I couldn't wait to have children so that I could do everything for them that the sperm donor didn't do for me.

My whole life changed in my new environment, which was filled with happiness, love and support. My mother and Vito (my true father) did everything in their power to make me happy and keep me grounded. Vito never wanted me to refer to him as my father out of respect for the actual sperm donor, but as time went on, he truly warmed up to the idea. I would, on occasion, see the sperm donor on weekends and some holidays, but the occasions were few and far between.

I guess this was where the actual normalcy came into play. Although I was enrolled in yet another school, I knew that this was it for me. No more moving around and making new friends. I wasn't an "A" student, but I was not dim-witted either. I had a decent amount of friends, some of whom I still have a very close relationship with. I was always smiling and very happy. I was a typical girl. I listened to and respected my extremely strict mother and kept a curfew until the day I got married.

I met my first serious boyfriend, "Neil," when I was fourteen, and I married him eleven years later. I didn't really have much dating experience, to say the least. I thought everything about our relationship was normal, but I didn't have anything to compare it to. Most of my friends were single or dating non-exclusively, so I spent most of my time with Neil.

Neil was two years older and never had a curfew. I, on the other hand, was not allowed out on school nights. I had to be home by 10:00 p.m. on the weekends—that didn't even happen until a year after we were dating. Neil had a lot of free time to go out and do whatever he wanted. It was almost like he didn't have a girlfriend and had a lot of fun on my watch. He was out almost every night, partying like a rock star with his friends. I was powerless; I couldn't hang out with him because I wasn't allowed. The day after it happened, mutual friends would tell me all the crazy stories about the drunken debauchery that went on. We fought a lot over such insignificant things that seemed so important at the time.

I have never been arrested, although I probably came close to it a few times. I had my fun growing up, partying and stuff like that, but nothing too crazy. I've always been a little silly and immature. I loved to have fun, and I always found myself in some kind of embarrassing situation. I tried very hard not to take anything too seriously; I loved my life, and I knew I was very blessed.

I graduated from high school and decided to go to a community college that was fifteen minutes away from my house. Most of my friends went away to college, and I wanted to be close to Neil, so it worked out well for me. I didn't have to share my time with my friends; I could now spend all of my time with my then-boyfriend.

Neil's drinking had gotten worse, and that escalated to experimenting with many other substances. We fought all the time about everything. He screwed up a lot at work and wasn't able to hold down a job. With that, his driver's license was suspended; he had no credit and barely ever had any money. The sad part was that Neil was super-intelligent and very talented. He had so much potential, and I wasn't ready to give up on him. I knew he had it in him to be a success, and I did whatever I could to help him.

I loved his family very much. They embraced me as if I was their child. They knew that I was having a hard time with Neil, and they would fight with him because they knew he was mistreating me. As time went on, my mother opened up to my relationship, and our families started spending a lot of time together, especially on the weekends. Neil's father was an excellent cook, so I looked forward to Sunday dinner every weekend. It was also a safe haven; whenever we were with his family, everything was good. After dinner ended was another story. I would have to go home, and he would have a nice buzz going on from the evening cocktails. He couldn't wait to get rid of me so that he could be on his way with his friends, "partying."

I was twenty-one and had been spending most of my days

taking care of Neil. Out of sheer frustration, his parents threw him out of their house, and he rented apartments with his friends. That meant I became his mother. I would make sure he went to work and paid his bills. I had to register and insure his cars because he had no driver's license and was driving around illegally. I bailed him out of jail several times due to traffic infractions or bar fights. What was I getting myself into?

I was growing tired of being put on the back burner. His apartment was party central almost every night. Since I graduated from high school and was now attending college, my mother upped my curfew to 12:00 a.m. I could only control what he was doing until midnight. After I went home, all hell would break loose. I was anxious all the time, worrying about what he was doing. I had to do something because I couldn't go on with my life like this. I knew that I eventually wanted to get married and have children. By the looks of my situation, I wasn't sure that Neil was going to make it to 30. He was reckless and had no boundaries. So what did I do? I gave him an ultimatum. "If you don't straighten out your act and make some kind of commitment to me, then I want to break up!"

Within a week of that conversation, he proposed to me. He replaced the roof on his parents' house to get the money for a ring. He literally took me to a jewelry store, left me in the car, ran into the store, bought the ring, came back to the car with the box in his hand and asked me to marry him. What did I do? I said yes!

I was engaged and miserable. Neil hadn't changed one bit, but he promised me that by the time our wedding neared, he would be 100 percent clean. I held on to his words, and in the meantime, I prepared for our wedding. My mother was thrilled. This was a dream come true for her, and she loved every second that we spent shopping for gowns and wedding accessories. Of course the sperm donor stepped up to the plate and said he was going to pay for the wedding; being the fool that I was, I believed him, and I went on planning my wedding. Neil had absolutely no interest whatsoever in the wedding plans. He couldn't have cared less, and that really upset me.

Our wedding was nearing, and the sperm donor never seemed to disappoint; he had received some kind of letter from the Child Support Bureau stating that he had to pay my mother several thousand dollars in previously owed child support. We had a huge fight, and the sperm donor said that if my mother didn't drop the charges, he wouldn't pay for the wedding. Guess what? Two months before my wedding, the sperm donor backed out. Nice!

Now I was left to pick up the pieces. I didn't have the money to cover the wedding expenses at all, so I was pretty much screwed. To add insult to injury, my soon-to-be sister-in-law's husband passed away. That was the first time that I had ever experienced loss. I loved my sister-in-law so much that it tore my heart out of my chest to see her suffer and be in so much mental agony. I didn't think things could possibly get worse, but they did. My pre-wedding situation should have been an omen not to get married.

My mother and Vito, my real father, came to the rescue and paid for the entire wedding. I couldn't believe it! I was so overwhelmed and thankful for their generosity. September 7, 1996 was the big day, and it was here. I can't explain how weird I felt that morning. I was so sad, and I couldn't put my finger on why. A big part of me was upset that I was leaving my parents' home, but something else was going on inside of me. It was my wedding day; I should have been happy. This wasn't the way it was supposed to be; it was the next step in my life. When I told my mother, she chalked it up to pre-wedding jitters.

I cried the whole way to the church in the limousine. When my parents walked me down the aisle, I didn't want to let go, but I had to. The sperm donor didn't even show his face in the church. It didn't matter much; this was my wedding day, and I was marrying Neil. After that day, everything was going to change. No more lies, no more drugs, no more partying. This was the start of a clean slate.

Unfortunately nothing changed, not even for our wedding day. It was a beautiful reception, and everything was perfect, but this wasn't a wedding; it was a huge, extremely expensive party. I tried to be optimistic and hoped that our wedding night was his last hurrah, but in my heart, I knew it wasn't. After the wedding, Neil disappeared with his friends and went to a bar, showing up fifteen minutes before we were to leave for our honeymoon at 6:30 in the morning. I was sad when I left my mother in the airport; I got choked up and cried in her arms as she said goodbye. This was my new life; I was a married woman now.

The honeymoon was over before it even began. Everything remained status quo in Neil's life, except for the fact that he had a live-in maid. Exploring my newly found freedom was fun in the beginning; I loved coming home from work and preparing dinner. I'd put my feet up on the coffee table and just relax, watching television with my dog, Toto. There was no curfew, and I pretty much answered to myself. But the umbilical cord was not severed, it was just stretched. My mother literally lived two minutes away, and that was just how I wanted it. The sperm donor was completely removed from the equation; I hadn't spoken to him since he backed out of my wedding. Neil's parents weren't too far from us, either; they lived a town away.

We were newlyweds, so naturally the next question on everyone's mind was, "When are you guys going to have a baby?"

We certainly were not ready to have children yet, and the thought scared me to death. I was having a hard enough time taking care of my dog let alone a baby. My goal was to save up enough money to eventually make a down payment on a house. We had a pretty decent head start from the gifts we received at our wedding. Neil wanted to start his own construction company, and I agreed to help him by putting everything in my name (lumber accounts, car, work truck, etc.) because he had no credit. He was extremely talented and did beautiful work, so I was confident that he would be a success. With the both of us working full-time, I hoped we would save enough by the time our lease was up the following year to buy a house. I took the money from the wedding, tucked it away in a savings account and refused to touch it until we were ready to buy a home.

However, things were quickly deteriorating beneath the surface. Come Friday night each week, our apartment became a local bar. By the time I got home from work at 5:10 p.m., my apartment was filled with booze, cigarette smoke and people. Don't get me wrong, I did enjoy hanging out with friends, but not every weekend in my apartment. I wanted to enjoy my new marriage and have some privacy sometimes, especially after working all week. We weren't saving any money at all; we were actually struggling to make our bills. I was stressed out all the time. I fought with Neil about the constant partying and rampant substance abuse that he was displaying almost every day. He wasn't getting paid as much as he expected because he missed work all of the time—hangovers. He lied to me constantly, and to make matters worse, the nest egg that I thought we had was completely depleted. He went through all the money in a matter of months. This was before ATMs and check cards were popular, so I just assumed the money was always there, never looking at the bank statements. As for the checking account, we never had a high balance because we never had a surplus of money, so whenever we got those statements, I would just rip them up and toss them into the trash. The only reason I had checked the statement that time was because we had bounced a check. When I saw the balance was less than $1000, I almost had a stroke. I was furious because he made up some crazy story that someone was stealing money from our account, and of course, I believed him. I went barging into the bank, accusing them of not protecting my account. To my utter shock, they told me that Neil was in there almost every day, withdrawing money. I was devastated, and after that, everything changed drastically for the worse.

We celebrated our one-year anniversary struggling to get by and fighting all the time. His substance abuse problem didn't get better; it got much worse. Along with that came all the lies, and I just couldn't trust him. It is almost impossible to maintain a relationship if there is no trust, not to mention the fact that Neil was an emotional cripple. He never wanted to do anything with me unless involved partying and getting drunk. I spent so much of my time with my mother and my friends Stacy and Kerri. This was not the way I wanted our marriage to be.

I figured an easy solution would be for us to move to another town; this way, our apartment wouldn't be so close to all of his friends, and they would all find a new hangout. Well that plan completely backfired because they all followed us to our new home. I was totally miserable. There were nights that we would get into arguments, and I would drive over to my parents' house. I would never go in; I would just sit in front the house, sobbing. I didn't know what to do. If I went in the house, then all of the secrets would be exposed, and I didn't know if I was ready for that. I wanted our marriage to work, so I had to help myself.

I started to see a therapist, but Neil refused to go. He didn't feel that there was anything wrong. Through the therapist, I got involved in a support group for addicts and their families. He refused to participate in that as well. I kept hitting road blocks everywhere I turned, and I couldn't handle it anymore. I wanted to be happy and have a normal life with a house, children and a dog. I wasn't asking for too much. The way things were going, I couldn't see any of that in our future, and I was only twenty-six. After a million ultimatums, nothing changed. He didn't want the help because he didn't think he had a problem. You can lead a horse to water, but you can't make him drink it. I loved him, but I couldn't save him. Our relationship was different now; I loved him like he was my son, not my husband, and that wasn't good. After all of my threats backfired on me, I had to go. I knew I deserved so much better than I was settling for. At that point in our relationship, I was holding on because I loved his family so much, and I knew that things would be different if I left. I just couldn't hold on anymore. I was crying at work, and it was affecting everything that I did. Four days after our two-year anniversary, I left and never looked back.

I had to face the music and tell my parents everything, especially because their home was the only place I could go. In the beginning, they didn't believe me until they spoke with Neil's family. They confirmed everything that I was telling my parents. It was over, and I was finally pushed to the point of no return. It seemed so sudden to my parents, but I had been silently fighting this battle for a very long time. I got a lawyer and filed for a divorce right away. My next obstacle was figuring out how I was going to cover all of my debt. All of our personal bills were piling up alongside of his business accounts, none of which had been paid. Neil said he wouldn't help me with the bills unless I came back, and that just was not an option.

I had no choice but to file for bankruptcy because I couldn't afford to keep up with everything. My life had reached an all time low, but I was on my way to happier days.

I was a twenty-six-year-old bankrupt divorcée living in my parents' house. The last thing on my mind was getting involved in another relationship. I hated men and was actually considering a non-sexual lesbian existence. As I mentioned earlier, I had been dating Neil since I was 14, so I hadn't been on a date in a very long time. I was sure that dating in your late 20s was a little different than dating as a teenager, so I was a bit apprehensive about the idea. I would go out to bars and clubs with my closest friends, but it was extremely uneventful and sometimes scary. The single life may seem appealing to some, but to me it was frightening. There were so many jerks out there with absolutely nothing to offer. Mr. Right is a hard find at 2:00 a.m. at a club.

I found love where I least expected it, and it knocked me off my feet. My brother Michael worked in the service unit at a local car dealership and had gotten me a job in the finance department about a year before I left Neil. I knew most of his friends from work, but I never paid them any mind. Around the time I separated from Neil, my brother's friend Joey was going through a rough time with his girlfriend, so we would compare notes. I had known Joe for a few years already, and he would come by our house to hang out with Michael. Joey was really sweet and very cute, but I never thought of him in "that" way. Besides he was totally not my type. Joey was a "Guido" all the way with big muscles, multiple piercing in his ears, perfect clothes, gold chains, and always smelled like some strong cologne. He was a ladies' man, always with some pretty girl and definitely more experienced on the dating scene than I was. I was used to the deadhead, pot-smoking, hippie type who couldn't care less about clothing let alone hygiene.

After a while, I started to see through Joey's womanizing persona. It was all an act. Inside, he was a caring, compassionate person who was much more intelligent than he let on. I wasn't looking for love, but it certainly found me. I could talk to him for hours on end about anything. And he would make me laugh until I cried. I started to feel something that I never felt before. I had butterflies in my stomach every time I saw him. Joey gave me a reason to go to work and get dressed up; he made me feel pretty, and that was something I hadn't sensed in a long time. I knew I had to pace myself because I had just separated from Neil and didn't need more drama in my life, but I was very intrigued by Joey.

By Christmas of 1998, I was legally separated and dating Joey. Some would say that I moved on very quickly, but Joey invoked feelings in me that I never felt before. He turned my world around and showed me what true love really was—it's so corny, but it's true. Our relationship was great; I finally met my match, and we loved to be together. He was actually interested in what I had to say. He cared about how my day was and vice versa. We communicated well, and that was important to me. Joey and Neil were polar opposites. For starters, Joey had a valid driver's license, credit cards and a bank account. It was refreshing to drive around with him without worrying that we were going to get pulled over by a cop, or that he would get arrested. Joey was going to college; he had his own apartment and car. I was the dirt bag who lived with her parents, bankrupt with no bank account. He was ambitious and wanted to have a career in law enforcement. We went out to dinner all the time and tried new things. He was spontaneous and would plan road trips for us out of the blue to Montauk or Atlantic City. No matter what we did, we had fun with no stress or arguing involved. We were truly in love.

There were no real problems, except for the fact that I was a bit of a worrier, but I will get into that later.

On Christmas morning, 1999, Joey totally surprised me and proposed. I was shocked and completely elated. I said yes! This time around, there was no hesitation; I knew I was doing the right thing, and I couldn't have been happier. Planning the wedding was awesome, and Joey helped with everything. He actually had an opinion. We tied the knot on March 31, 2001. This time, I cried as I walked down aisle because I found my soul mate. I was never more positive about anything else in my life. We had a big beautiful wedding with all of our close friends and family, minus the sperm donor. A few months after our wedding, we made a down payment on the house of our dreams and moved in with my mother and Vito until we went to closing. Everything just seemed to fall into place.

On September 11, 2001, the unimaginable happened, and I felt the world was coming to an end. In a matter of seconds, everything changed. I watched the news coverage constantly; it consumed my days. I was obsessed! I was anxious and worried all day long about the "next attack." I couldn't understand why everyone else around me wasn't as concerned. I was truly freaking out. Joey banned me from watching the news because I would get myself so worked up that I would cry. OCD was really beginning to rear its evil head, but I didn't know it. Putting aside all of my panic really made me put things into perspective, and I realized how precious life is.

By October 2001, we moved into our new home. My husband got a job working as a police officer in Suffolk County, and I was working for a national auto group as a Human Resources Manager. We both loved our jobs, and everything was falling into place. The next step for us was to start our family. It was something that I dreamt of since I was a little girl.

During the same month we moved into our house, I found out that I was pregnant! The due date was July 11, 2002. Joey and I weren't really planning to have a child so soon, but if it happened, that was okay too. Oddly enough I had taken three home pregnancy tests and they all came back negative. The fourth test was the charm. We were both excited and scared at the same time.

After the initial shock, I couldn't wait to be a mother. I wanted to tell everyone, but I held back. "They" say, it's bad luck to tell anyone you're pregnant until after the first trimester, so we kept it a secret from everyone except our closest friends and family, and that even made me a little worried. "What if" I jinxed my pregnancy?

After the first trimester was over, I told everyone I was having a baby. It didn't matter who they were, or if I even knew them. I did everything by the book. I took my prenatal vitamins, ate extremely healthily and got plenty of sleep. I purchased the book *What to Expect When You are Expecting* and revered it like it was my Bible. I literally carried it with me wherever I went. I also joined an online mother to be website, which gave me an intricate description of how I should be feeling and the month-by-month growth of the fetus. I found myself obsessing (I will take that word to a new level) over every little thing in the book. I was also listening to everyone's advice. *Everyone* had an opinion! Don't eat tuna, don't eat cold cuts, don't wear high heel shoes, and don't stand in front of a microwave. My favorite comment was "don't eat maraschino cherries; the baby will get brain damage." I don't know if that's true or not; it sounds a little crazy, but at the time, I believed it. I heard things like, "if you're carrying low, you must be having a boy," or "you're face is changing, so you must be having a girl!" Who comes up with this stuff? Needless to say, I was a bundle of nerves. It was all that I thought about all day long. I would go on the computer to see if there was any merit to these crazy comments, and when I couldn't find the answer, I would call my OB. All that I wanted was a healthy baby.

We couldn't wait to find out the sex of the baby. Joey and I decided that we wanted to know right away. Of course the critics have to give their opinion about that too. "It's wrong to find out the sex of the baby"; "Don't you want to be surprised?"; "Those things are never right anyway." The way Joe and I saw it, we were going to be surprised whether we found out at five months or waited until the day the baby was born. The verdict was in: *it's a girl!* Maybe . . .

My bump was growing, and I loved every month. I even kept a diary. I was out shopping every week for new, trendy maternity clothes. Still, every day I worried something could go wrong. Would our baby be born okay? Would the baby be born still, have down syndrome, or some other birth defect? I was sure that was something every mom-to-be thought about.

I was so self-conscious! Joey and I decided to stop having sex when I was in my sixth month. It was just way too uncomfortable for both of us. Joey was afraid that having sex would somehow harm the baby, and he feared that he would feel the baby moving inside of me. I thought he was going to stop loving me because of the lack of intimacy, and I looked like an ogre. Although I was so happy to be pregnant, I had never felt so ugly before in my life.

As I entered my seventh month, I was still working full-time all the way in Westbury, which was about an hour away from my house. One day while I was at work, I had these horrible pains in my stomach, and I ran to the bathroom. I felt like I had to move my bowels, badly! I sat on the bowl for about fifteen minutes and nothing was happening. I went back into my office, but my stomach was killing me. I felt as if I was going to soil myself, so I ran back into the bathroom. Nothing, again. The sensation was there for me to keep pushing but nothing was coming out at all. I was so uncomfortable that it was hard for me to sit down. I was beginning to panic. Was this a possible sign of early labor? Were these contractions?

I called Joe at work and told him what was going on, and he told me to come home right away. Right away was difficult when I was an hour away, but I was going to move as fast as possible. Like I said before, sitting was tough. Now at this stage, I was about 200 pounds and was driving a Toyota Solara, which is not a very big car, not to mention my sitting problem. I got on the Parkway and drove into bumper-to-bumper traffic. I thought I was going to have a stroke. The sensation was getting worse. I had this huge belly in front of me that was hitting the steering wheel because I couldn't put my ass down on the seat. I had this agonizing look of pain on my face. There were people driving past staring at the freak show that was going on in my car.

Finally, the parkway opened up, and I was able to drive faster. At this point I was bouncing up and down in the seat like a child that has to go to the bathroom. I felt like I was going to throw up because the pain was so bad. I finally made it home, and Joe was already there. I busted through the door pulling my pants down before I even made it into the bathroom. I almost broke the toilet seat because I pounced on it so hard. And, nothing. I pushed and pushed to no avail. My belly was rock hard and I could feel the baby writhing around. Something was going on in there, and she wasn't happy about it.

Joey came into the bathroom to find me on the floor, naked, rocking back and forth on all fours. He didn't even say a word; he just shook his head in disbelief. I was hysterical. I thought that I was going into labor. Maybe the baby wanted to come out of my ass, because that is what it felt like. What else could it be? Hemorrhoids?

Joey got the doctor on the phone and he told us to come right in. Back to the car! Being that I couldn't sit like a normal person, I sat in the passenger seat facing the seat on my knees. We got to the doctor's office and it was packed. Lucky for me they took me in immediately.

I was in the examining room, and the nurse asked me to sit up on the table. That was problematic since I couldn't sit. I was so antsy and fidgety; I think she thought I was on speed or something. So she made me take my pants and underwear off and stand there with the giant napkin covering me until the doctor was ready to see me. About two minutes later, Dr. Jean came in the room and was ready for business. I was in tears and couldn't stand still. Imagine having the feeling that you have to go to the bathroom badly but it lasts for three hours. It was agonizing. I couldn't imagine what he was going to do to help me. I had a feeling I was going to wind up in the hospital or giving birth. He assured me that I wasn't going into labor, and he asked me to get on the table and lay down.

There I was looking up at the ceiling. I couldn't see what was going on because my belly was in the way. I saw him put his examining gloves on with a little lube and then I saw stars. I jumped off that exam table and burst out the door into the bathroom (with no pants on). I didn't care who saw what. I think that I dropped five pounds that day. It looked like a football in the toilet bowl. The instant relief that I felt was overwhelming. The next dilemma was unclogging the toilet. My humiliated husband sat in the waiting room with everyone else, all of whom witnessed the whole act followed by me walking out of the bathroom followed by the nurses with a plunger and gloves. Never a dull moment.

I stopped working and went on maternity leave in the beginning of my eighth month. Joey and I agreed that I was getting way too close to my due date to be working so far away from home. It was June and it was *hot!* When I had become pregnant, I was 130 pounds, and by my eighth month, I was about 210 pounds. I was big. Everything was huge—my nose looked like a bubble, my feet grew two sizes bigger and my boobs were tremendous. I started to look like Princess Fiona from Shrek; the only difference was that I wasn't green.

In my eighth month I started taking Lamaze classes. I don't think Joey was as excited about the classes as I was, but he came anyway. That is where I met one of the five angels that would save my life; Lori, the Lamaze instructor. She was so full of energy and life and her smile brightened up the whole room.

The first day of class we watched a video of a mother giving birth. I remember that the mom had a huge smile on her face like she was getting a massage or something. I couldn't believe how graphic the video was. Not only was it graphic, it was really gross. It looked like a murder scene; I couldn't believe the amount of blood she lost. I glanced over at Joe from time-to-time and he looked like he was going to throw up. Not to mention the woman's pubic area was completely out of control. I had to give myself a mental note to shave my own "area" a little; I hadn't seen it in such a long time. I only hoped I would be able reach. From the looks of the woman on the video, she never shaved—ever!

By July, I was ready to pop! My belly button came out about five inches; it was freakish. The baby moved constantly. I was getting elbow jabs and drop kicks from the inside. This baby was going to be a kickboxer or a soccer star. It was truly bizarre and extremely uncomfortable, but I loved it anyway.

That year the 4th of July was one of the hottest days of the summer. My mother had this great idea to go walking around an art show in town. I swear it was like walking around on the sun. I thought I was going to go into labor right in the middle of the street. I was having contractions here and there, but nothing to be concerned about. I had seen some old friends there, and they didn't even recognize me. How could they? It was the new 200 pound me; Princess Fiona. After that excursion, I decided it was time to stay indoors until the baby was born.

With all my new spare time indoors, I started getting the nursery ready for the baby's arrival. The furniture was delivered and assembled. Joey and I had so much fun decorating. It was very pretty and delicate, but it was a sage green color, just in case "she" came out a "he."

My OB said that I would know when the baby was coming, and boy was he right. We had so many false alarms, but on July 15th at 5:00 a.m., the most horrible pain I had ever felt awakened me. I knew this was it! There was no mistaking it, I was in labor. I told Joey to get his ass out of bed and get me to the hospital.

Whoever says childbirth is a beautiful thing is a liar. I don't care what anybody says, it is an extremely painful experience. This was definitely not what I expected. As soon as we got to the hospital, I wanted an epidural, and no one was giving it to me. I had to wait until I was dilated more; at that point, I was only three centimeters. The contractions were so bad that I thought I was going to bite my tongue off.

I had Joey and my mother with me in the birthing room trying to keep me calm. My husband looked totally petrified, so he wasn't a lot of help. My mom was a trooper; she did whatever she could to relax me. To make matters worse, the night before, I went out to dinner with my husband and my parents and had steak fajitas, resulting in the worst indigestion.

The nurse decided it would be best for me to walk around a little to help the process along. I wanted to punch the nurse right in the head. I couldn't even stand up straight, and the medical staff wanted me to walk around. So there I was, walking around the maternity ward, wearing that horrible gown they gave me. My whole ass was exposed because they never close properly. I had one hand trying to keep the gown closed and the other was pulling the IV pole. All the while, I was doubling over in pain from the contractions every three minutes. I walked around for two minutes and called it quits.

On my way back to the room, I started to feel really nauseous. Steak Fajitas + Labor = Big Problem.

The next thing I knew, I was throwing up all over the place. There was steak, peppers, lettuce, tortilla chips and refried beans all over the room. I can still remember the look on Joey's face; I think he was waiting for my head to start spinning around. My poor Joey looked like he was in a state of shock.

I think I would rather be skinned alive and thrown in alcohol than go through pain like that again. After that little episode, they cleaned me up, mopped the floors, sanitized the walls and then they decided it was time to give me the epidural. About five seconds after the needle pinched my spine, I felt relief. Finally I got a reprieve from the agony.

From there, I thought it would be smooth sailing. My husband got the color back into his face and started to talk again. We all watched TV, waiting for I don't know what to happen. A few hours had gone by; there were nurses and doctors coming in and out. They gave me a catheter, which was kind of awkward and very distressing. Then I felt this really uncomfortable pressure, almost like I had to move my bowels. Something was happening, and I didn't want it to happen on the bed or in front of my husband.

I called the nurses to come in and check me out. Within seconds they were getting me ready to push. Apparently the baby wanted out! Joey was directly behind me, rubbing my head; my mom was holding my left leg, and the nurse was holding my right; the doctor, who wasn't my OB, told me to start the breathing techniques that I learned in Lamaze class. Lamaze class? I couldn't remember my first name let alone what I learned in Lamaze class. I forgot everything!

It was a very surreal feeling, being naked with my legs spread wide open and a bunch of people focusing in on my crotch—and I never got a chance to shave! I started off on my back, pushing for a while, then they had me move to my right side, and then to my left. I was pushing, but nothing was coming out. The final straw was having me push on all fours. Talk about strange. I had all kinds of tubes coming out of me; my stomach was big, and my boobs were all over the place. I just wanted this whole situation to be over.

Finally the nurses got Dr. Jean. I can remember his face; it was pensive. Nobody said a word, but I knew right away that something was wrong. The doctors and nurses were scrambling all over the room. The nurse pulled up the apron and started putting iodine all over my stomach. Then, to my surprise, the nurse started shaving my pubic area (which I really needed and sort of appreciated).

They rushed me out of the birthing room and brought me right into this cold bright operating room. I was horrified, to say the least. My husband and mother were left behind in the birthing room. I didn't recognize any familiar faces. Was my worst fear coming true? Was I about to lose my baby? I started to cry; nobody was saying anything to me.

The nurses pulled my gown up and formed a curtain, blocking

my view from what was going on down below. There were big mirrors at every corner of the room, so I could see somewhat. Dr. Jean was standing right next to me and held my hand. He told me that the baby's heart rate went from 125 down to 45, and they had to do an emergency C-section. There was another doctor, an anesthesiologist, to my left. It seemed like they were both talking to me at the same time. I asked if everything was going to be okay but didn't get an answer. At the same time, the anesthesiologist was administering some medication, and within seconds, I was in another world.

I was in a horrible nightmare and wanted to wake up. I was falling in and out of consciousness, and I felt a lot of pressure on my abdomen. My whole body was being jerked around. I looked up at one of the mirrors and saw my insides laying on my chest. It was a big bloody mess. I could not believe what was going on.

Then it happened; the most amazing thing I had ever seen. My beautiful baby, Madison Andrea Isnardi, was born. I saw the nurses wiping her down and suctioning her mouth. I remember reaching out my arm toward her. I wanted to see her and hold her, but I was in a drug-induced stupor. I heard the nurses saying "Oh my God she is so beautiful."

Very weakly, I said, "My baby," as tears were pouring down my face.

One of the nurses held Madison in front of me and said, "Look at your beautiful baby." At that point, I didn't care what happened to me. I was just elated that she was okay, and she was more than okay. She was perfect.

I felt a presence behind me that I thought was my doctor. It turned out to be Joey. The scrubs they gave him to wear were three sizes too small on him. He looked ridiculous because they were so tight and short. It actually looked pretty funny, and I remember chuckling a bit. The nurse handed Madison to Joey, and he held her near my face. She was so beautiful; everything about her was angelic. And to top it off Madison actually had a smile on her face. Meanwhile, my guts were all exposed for everyone to see, and no one cared. It was like a gory horror movie. My friend, Dr. Anesthesiologist, returned with his needles, and before I knew it, I was unconscious once again.

I woke up in the hallway of the maternity ward about three hours later, although it felt like fifteen minutes. My mother, who was sitting in the chair right next to me, was coming in and out of focus. I felt as high as a kite; I almost forgot where I was. Then I asked her what had happened and if the baby was okay. She gave me all the details and assured me that Madison was fine. Joey had taken her into the waiting room to show her off to the family. I fell asleep again and woke up in my room about an hour later.

My hospital room was filled with flowers, balloons and people. I was feeling no pain; the doctors had me on some heavy-duty drugs. I think that I was babbling incoherently, but nobody cared. Everyone was focused on Madison. That was okay with me; I just wanted to sit there. I was so exhausted and overwhelmed. At one point I started to throw up, and nobody noticed. Finally my mother saw me drooling all over myself and helped clean me up. She handed me a bedpan to throw up in and went back to Madison. The compassion was just overwhelming.

Dr. Jean came by to explain everything that happened, and that I would be in the hospital for about a week to recover. Madison was very healthy and alert, so I was thrilled. I couldn't have asked for a better result.

When I held Madison in my arms for the first time, it was like magic. I couldn't describe the feeling. I loved her so much; I just started sobbing uncontrollably. I wanted to hold on to that feeling forever. I didn't want to let go. Then the nurse came in and took her away. I couldn't keep her in the room with me because I couldn't get up to care for her as a result of the surgery and the stitches. It was for the best because I needed the sleep.

The nurse wheeled her away, and once again, I started to cry. I missed her before she left the room. Now I wanted everyone else out. I just wanted to spend some time with Joey. He stayed as late as he possibly could. Security threw him out. I was so drugged up that I just passed out. I don't even remember Joey leaving.

The nurse awoke me at 3:00 a.m. It was time to take my temperature, check my vitals and give me more medication. I was pissed; I just wanted to sleep, but I needed the meds. I was in so much pain; my whole abdomen felt like it was on fire. All that I could think about was my little baby down the hall. I wanted to be with her so badly, but I couldn't. So I started to cry. Again. I worried that she wasn't being cared for properly. What if she was crying, or what if the hospital caught on fire? How was I going to help her? I figured it was my natural maternal reaction to feel that way, although it was excessive. Finally the meds started to kick in, and I was back in a coma.

At 6:00 a.m. the nurse was back, picking and prodding and poking. Now I was up, and all I wanted to do was see Madison. The nurse told me that they would bring her in at about 8:00 a.m. So now what? I was bored, and there was nothing to watch on the television but the news. Luckily Joey showed up at about 6:30 a.m.

We talked about the whole ordeal that happened the day before because it was a bit of a blur to me. Joey told me how worried he and my mother were when they took me into the operating room. He told me he was afraid that he was going to lose me. I realized how much he really loved me. After all the throwing up and watching me try to push the baby out, then seeing my guts pulled out of me, he still loved me. All 208 pounds of me. To make matters worse, it seemed as if everything on me had swollen up. My nose now consumed my entire face, my fingers looked like sausage links, and my breasts were so inflated I thought they were going to burst.

At 8:00 a.m. the nurse wheeled the baby in. She looked like an oversized cocoon; she was so damn cute. It was time for us to learn how to feed the baby. It seemed pretty simple. The only problem was just how much and when. Madison was a hungry little sucker; she could pound those little two-ounce bottles down with no trouble. Her lips were perfect, and she would pucker them from time to time; it was so adorable. Joey and I ate up every second of her.

Then the nurse came back in and said that it was time for me to try and stand up for the first time since the surgery. She was removing the catheter and wanted me to move my bowels. I could barely sit up on my own, and now they want me to stand up, walk and go to the bathroom! Well, let me tell you, I think the entire hospital heard me scream. Just lifting my body up and off the bed was a nightmare. It felt like my whole uterus was going to fall out onto the floor. It took me about ten minutes to walk five feet. I practically jumped onto the toilet bowl so I could sit down.

It is amazing what comes out of the body after a C-section. It looked like a blood bath in the toilet. I swore my intestines fell out. I was so petrified that I pulled that little "in case of emergency string" next to the toilet. Three nurses came running in just to tell me that that kind of blood loss and clotting was normal. Normal? I thought I was going to need a blood transfusion. This certainly was not the way I imagined my birthing experience to be. Nobody warns you about any of the other things that could possibly happen if you can't deliver a baby naturally. I was very disenchanted to say the least.

By the second night, I was allowed to keep Madison in the room with me. I would just stare at her in the bassinet and sob! I loved her more than I thought I could ever love anything. It was so overwhelming and absolutely amazing. Childbirth was not beautiful, but the end result definitely was.

The most embarrassing day of my life, July 18th, was my fourth day in the hospital. I still had not moved my bowels, even though they had given me several laxatives and a lot of prune juice. According to my doctor, I was filled with gas from the procedure. They were going to have to perform a procedure called a "Murphy Drip." This is a slow, continuous, drop-by-drop administration of saline solution into the rectum and sigmoid colon. Great!

The procedure is supposed to flush my system by letting all the gas out. Well! It was Joey, two nurses, and myself in my room. The door was wide open; the only thing blocking me from everyone else in the maternity ward was a thin cotton curtain. I had no idea what to expect. In went the tube, and in a matter of seconds, I started letting out gas. It was loud and long. It went on for about three minutes. Three minutes of pure loud flatulence. I saw people walking down the hallway past my room gasping. I couldn't care less at that point. I found myself apologizing to my husband because I knew he was mortified. In the twelve years we have been together, I have yet to hear him pass gas. There I was, causing a scene as a result of my gas. I think I could've won an award for my performance in the *Guinness Book of World Records*. My bowels moved just fine after that.

On the fifth day, it was time to go home. From the moment I woke up, I was crying; I was so emotional. I was hoping that the feeling was going to pass. This was a first for me, and I had no idea what to feel or expect. The nurses came in and handed me a folder that was about three inches thick filled with a million different pamphlets and documents in different shapes and sizes with information on formula and baby stuff. I figured that I would look over everything when I arrived home. Then they gave me a quick lesson on bathing the baby and that was it. I got Madison dressed in a special little outfit for her first homecoming while I waited for the discharge papers. The whole time, I was sobbing just thinking about her, imagining her all grown up and not wanting to be with me anymore. It sounds ridiculous being that she was only five days old, but I was crying. All I wanted to do was cherish every moment I had with her. I just loved her so much. The most disturbing thing was the fact that all the nurses in the maternity ward saw me crying and never questioned why I was so sad. These were all trained professionals working in the maternity unit. Did they not care or had they not been trained properly on the signs of postpartum depression?

My worrying intensified from the moment I was wheeled out of the hospital. The nurses assisted Joey, helping him put Madison in the car seat securely. She was so tiny, only nineteen inches long and seven-pounds six-ounces. She looked like a little jellybean. Joey drove five miles an hour the whole way home. Your whole perspective changes when you have a child. I sat in the backseat holding on to the car seat, as if that was going to help. I just wanted to get home where it was safe, away from all the crazy drivers on the road. I was still crying. I couldn't believe how much love I was feeling. It was overpowering.

Finally, we arrived at our house. My mother was there already tidying things up. We walked through the door; the new family. I didn't know what to do with myself; I was very anxious. What if the baby started to choke? What if she didn't like me? What if I couldn't stop her from crying? I was still a little sore, and I couldn't really do much because of all the stitches. So I would just lie around, holding Madison. I loved everything about her. When she fell asleep, I just stared at her in the bassinet and cried (again).

The first week home was filled with visitors and phone calls. It was very nice, but I really just wanted some alone time with my husband and Madison. I assumed sooner or later all the well-wishing would die down, and our lives would go back to some kind of normalcy.

By the second week at home, I was a professional. This mommy stuff was easy. Madison went to sleep at 9:00 p.m. and woke at 7:00 a.m. It was like a dream. I was "Supermom," and all that I was missing was my cape. I did it all; I changed her diapers, bathed her, and fed her. I didn't need or want any help from anyone, and I was only comfortable with my husband and me caring for the baby. As a matter of fact, I didn't want anyone to touch her or breathe near her. If new visitors came into the house, I would make them wash their hands and then use hand sanitizer. After the guests would leave, I would spray the entire room with Lysol. I would wash my hands all day long to the point that the skin was beginning to peel off.

I had my first appointment with my OB since the birth. I was so happy that I couldn't wait for Dr. Jean to see Madison. In my eyes, he saved her life, and I loved him for that. I brought her into the office and showed her off. I even brought her into the exam room because I didn't want her to be out of my sight for one second. Everything was healing properly, so I got the green light to go home and return in six weeks for another checkup.

I started waking up in the middle of the night to watch her sleep, just in case she stopped breathing in her bassinet. We had a movement sensor in the bassinet, but I didn't trust it. What if it stopped working? One night I actually put my makeup compact

Hell on Earth

I heard Joey walk in the door from work that evening at about 12:30 a.m. I pretended I was sleeping. I heard him talking to my mother, and she told him I was really tired and wanted to go to sleep. They said their goodbyes, and my mother left. My heart was pounding out of my chest because I was so anxious.

Joey came into the bedroom and put Madison in her bassinet. Normally I would lie near the bassinet. This time I would lie on the other side so Joey would be nearest to her. I totally ignored him; I just lay there with my eyes closed. My husband got undressed and came to bed.

As we lay there, I prayed to God that I would wake up and this would all go away. The thoughts that were going through my mind made no sense. I couldn't stop thinking about and visualizing Madison's little head jerking back the way it did.

Feelings of guilt that I hurt her where driving me crazy. I knew that she was fine, but the images playing in my head would take on a life of their own, like the one of her gasping for air. I had thoughts of her dying. It was just horrible. What was happening to me?

I woke at about 6:00 a.m., and everyone was still asleep. Something was wrong with me. I didn't feel better, that was most certain, I felt worse. The anxiety was overpowering and horrible thoughts were flooding my mind. I tried to close my eyes and go back to sleep. I felt as if I was losing my mind. I turned to Joey and hugged him with all I had. I was so scared trying to figure out what was going on. I went through the series of events that had gone on the past few days, and I couldn't think of anything. Nothing could justify the crazy thoughts. I didn't want to hurt my daughter. I would harm myself before I would do anything to her. She was my life. What was I going to do?

Two hours had gone by, and Madison woke up. I wasn't able to fall back asleep, and by that time, I was freaking out. The only thing that was in my favor was that Joey had the next two days off. I pretended that I was sleeping again, which forced Joey to wake up and take care of her.

Joey fed and changed Madison. At three weeks old, she didn't really do too much, so Joey placed her back in the bassinet. Normally, I would carry Madison everywhere around the house. This morning, I didn't. I stayed as far away from her as I possibly could, which made my husband very suspicious. I just lay in bed, paralyzed by fear and anxiety.

Joey asked me if I was feeling okay, and I told him that there was something wrong with me. Maybe I was coming down with something. I couldn't explain what was going on. After that conversation, I ran into the bathroom. I put the water on in the bathtub, sat on the floor and cried my eyes out. I felt like I was going to throw up, but I didn't. I wiped my tears and walked back into the bedroom.

Joey asked if I wanted to have some breakfast. The last thing I wanted to do was eat. I was sick to my stomach. My heart was pounding through my chest. I felt restless and unable to organize my thoughts. Was I going crazy?

I walked into the kitchen, and my thoughts were out of control. Even though Madison lay safely in her bassinet in the other room, I was having crazy thoughts of harm befalling her. Everything posed a threat. I looked at the oven, and a thought popped into my mind that she was in there. I looked at the knives on the counter, and another thought popped into my head that she was possibly stabbed with one of them. Every time I tried to stop the thoughts, they came on stronger, and the anxiety worsened. Who thinks this way? I wanted to bash my head into the wall to try and stop the thoughts. Nothing worked. I was clueless. I knew one thing: I did *not* want to be left alone.

I wanted to scream. I wanted to talk to someone, anyone. I needed help. If I told Joey about my thoughts, he would have me put in jail or in a mental hospital. He would take Madison away from me. I said nothing.

Joey went into the bedroom and started to get changed. I remember running in the room and asking him where he was going. He couldn't leave me; I was on the verge of a mental breakdown. Our computer was broken, so he was dropping it off at a nearby Radio Shack for repairs, which was literally three minutes away. The situation went something like this:

Wendy: I am coming with you!

Joey: Why? I will be back in five minutes.

Wendy Isnardi

WENDY: I need to get out of the house. It's a beautiful day. I could use some fresh air!

[However, it was about 100 degrees outside with 100 percent humidity.]

JOEY: Uh, okay. Change Madison, and let's go.

WENDY: No! I will leave her in her pajamas. Nobody is going to see her. Just grab her, and I will get the computer and put it in the car.

We were off; it was our first outing as a family. Joey got Madison and put her in her car seat. I got the computer and put it in the car. No questions asked. I sat in the backseat, petrified. Madison was smiling and cooing safely in her car seat. My thoughts were much different from the last car ride we had taken together coming home from the hospital. Thoughts and images of her falling out of her car seat and onto the pavement were racing through my head. I was shaking. I wanted to jump out of the car myself. When was this going to end, and what could I do to stop it?

Joey ran into Radio Shack with the computer. I wanted to go in with him, but he was literally just dropping it off. The three minutes he was in the store seemed eternal. I was panicking that Madison might start to cry, and I would have to help her. Sadly, just one day before, I was able to do all the normal things a mother should do. Now, I didn't even want to be alone with my own child. I just sat there in the backseat staring at my husband inside the store, watching his every move, waiting for him to get back in the car. I was tapping my foot up and down. I had so much nervous energy that I could feel the car moving with every tap.

Finally, Joey came back to the car. The computer wasn't going to be ready for a couple days. That really pissed me off because I wanted to see if I could go on the computer to research what was going on with me, and now I couldn't until I got my computer back.

Joey wanted to get something to eat for lunch. I wasn't hungry. The thought of food disgusted me. I hadn't eaten anything since dinner the night before, so we went to McDonald's, and I got a coffee. I just wanted to go home. I needed help; I needed to talk to someone. I figured that if I spoke to one of my friends who recently had a baby, maybe they could shed some light on the situation. I was so desperate.

As soon as I got home, I walked outside and called my friend Carrie, who had a two-year-old boy. We had a very open relationship, and I could talk to her about anything. But how? How do I tell her about my thoughts and the horrible way I was feeling? Normally our conversations were silly. We would talk about current events, sex and gossip. Rarely ever serious, but I had to talk to someone, and she was one of my few friends who had a child.

We chatted for a bit about nothing. I tried to giggle and laugh. Then she asked me how I was feeling. I tried my hardest to hold back the tears, but I couldn't help myself. I told her that I was feeling really strange, and that I couldn't stop crying. Carrie immediately stopped me and told me that she went through a very similar situation. She said she wanted to kill her husband and everyone else she came in contact with, and she couldn't stop crying. She proceeded to tell me that it was a hormonal thing, and I needed to make an appointment with my OB to get back on the birth control pill. I just needed to regulate my hormones. After a week of being on the pill, she went back to normal.

Was that it? Was that all I had to do? Go back on the pill? That seemed pretty simple. Now all I had to do was make it through the weekend and go to my OB on Monday to get back on the pill. This seemed pretty straightforward for that moment. Then the thoughts started up again, and I started questioning the conversation I had with Carrie. I never really told her what kind of thoughts I was having, and she didn't say she was really going through the same exact thing. All that I could hold on to for my own sanity was the possibility that going to the OB and getting back on the pill was going to help. It's all that I had.

I walked inside the house, and Joey was sitting at the kitchen table holding Madison. I needed to talk to him and tell him what was going on. At the very least, I needed to tell him what Carrie had just told me about the hormonal changes. I sat down and started to cry. I told him that I was not feeling like myself; I was overwhelmed and very sad. I explained that it was probably a hormonal thing, and I needed to see the doctor on Monday.

For a second, I thought that Joey was going to be mad and tell me to snap out of it, but he didn't; it was as if he understood. Joey suggested that I go through the folder of paperwork that I came home with from the hospital. Maybe there was something in there that could help me. I had thrown the folder in my night table as soon as I came home from the hospital. I didn't think that I would ever look through it, and eventually I would just dump it in the garbage. I busted into the night table, throwing everything about looking for the folder. The folder was three inches thick, and it was bulging with documents and pamphlets. There had to be something in the folder that could help me.

The folder contained:

Newborn Screening Program—information on
    immunizations
Important News For New Mothers About Your Baby's
    HIV Test
Three copies of the Certificate of Live Birth
Newborn Discharge Instructions

Hell on Earth

Echo-Screen Infant Hearing Report
Newborn Screening:
Discharge Notice, State of New York Department of
    Health—a letter from the commissioner about
    Medicaid and Child Health Plus
Hepatitis B Vaccine Pamphlet
Testing Your Newborn Baby's Health (a bookmark)
Babies Sleep Safest on Their Backs Pamphlet
Postpartum Discharge Instructions—information on
    medication, wound care, and follow up appointment
    with doctor
Mother and Infant Teaching Guide
Infant Care Information Guide—bathing your baby, cord
    care, circumcision, diaper rash, teething, infant colic,
    thrush, reflux, diarrhea and constipation

Now, I had been in the hospital for five days. I had a follow-up appointment with my OB/GYN a week after I was released, and all that I had to go by was a poorly copied article on emotions, stating that I needed professional attention if I feel I may be going through the baby blues or postpartum depression. There was nothing about frightening thoughts of harm, debilitating anxiety, crying hysterically all day long, not being able to care for myself or my newborn, fear of being alone, hopelessness and wanting to die to get relief from myself. I think those issues are a lot more important than four different guides on bottle-feeding and cord care. Oh! And how could I forget my "Testing Your Newborn Baby's Health" bookmark. I really needed that.

So I was in the same boat I was in before. Scared, hopeless and isolated from everything I knew. I didn't want to talk to anyone. I needed relief because the anxiety was unrelenting. Once again, I walked into the bathroom and turned the water on for the shower. I just sat in the bathroom for twenty minutes and cried my eyes out. I thought the noise from the shower would muffle my crying a little bit. I would find out later from my husband that the whole shower thing didn't work. Joey heard everything.

My mother called to see how I was feeling. I didn't want to talk to her at first, but Joey made me. As soon as I heard her voice, I started crying all over again. My mother couldn't get a word in. I just sobbed. I told her that there was something really wrong with me, and I needed to go see my doctor again. She asked me if I was sick, like if I had a cold (I wish), and I told her I wasn't. Putting the way I was feeling into words was hard. If I had a runny nose and a cough, I could say it was a cold; if I was throwing up nonstop, I could say it was a stomach virus. How do I explain extreme anxiety, severe depression, constant crying, fear of being alone, horrible thoughts, and sheer panic? So I just said, "I feel like I am going crazy! I want to run away from myself."

There was silence. Then she said, "Maybe you're going through the baby blues. I went through the baby blues after I gave birth to your brother. You are going to be fine. This is normal."

The baby blues? What I was going through was *not* the baby blues. Even the name baby blues sounded way too cute to describe the way I was feeling.

The Baby Blues:

Approximately 60-80 percent of women experience the baby blues. This term refers to a period of temporary moodiness which usually begins one to three days after delivery. Symptoms may include sadness, irritability, frustration, and fatigue. These symptoms come and go but usually disappear within a couple of days (or a maximum of two weeks). Although the new mom feels quite miserable, the baby blues are not considered to be true postpartum depression.[1]

I wish I was going through the baby blues. That would've been a treat in comparison. Almost like a vacation from what I was really going through. What I was going through was more like "baby black death," not baby blues.

My mother offered to come over, but I told her not to. I just wanted to sit in my room, cry and feel sorry for myself. Who knew when I was going to need her next? I didn't want to exhaust my resources just yet.

I spent the rest of the evening glued to Joey's hip. He took on all of the baby responsibilities, and I just stood in the background and watched, almost as if I wasn't supposed to be there. If Joey had to go to the bathroom, I would actually stand by the door until he would come out. I was so pathetic.

Time went by at a staggering pace. A minute seemed like an hour. I just wanted it to be Monday already so I could go to the doctor, and he could put me back on the birth control pill. I hoped that was the light at the end of the tunnel. It was the only bit of hope I had to hold on to. I couldn't wait to go to bed, wake up and get Sunday over with.

When it was finally time for us to go to bed, I lay there with tears streaming down my face. I was praying to God again, in desperation. I begged for his forgiveness for, I don't know what, but I needed his help. Then I turned to Joey and asked him if we could go to church in the morning. His reply was, "Sure, if that's what you want to do."

I almost fell off the bed. I was in shock. At that point, I realized

1. http://www.postpartumny.org/whatisPPD.htm

that Joey was very worried about me. Normally if I even mentioned the word "church" he would laugh hysterically at me. My husband is *not* a religious person, at all. Now he said, "Sure, if that's what you want to do!" So I just closed my eyes and tried to go to sleep.

Sunday arrived with no changes. I think I was feeling worse. My husband stepped right into character and took care of Madison. Joey fed, bathed, and dressed her for our outing to church. I just threw anything on and pulled my hair back into a ponytail. The one task I did accomplish was filling Madison's diaper bag with all of the essentials and preparing some extra bottles. As I prepared the bottles, horrible thoughts were flying through my head. Did I put sanitized water in her bottle? Was the water contaminated? Did I accidentally put something else in the bottle other than formula, like medication or some kind of poison? What if she got sick from the bottles that I was preparing? I wanted to bash my head into the counter to stop the thoughts. The more I tried to stop them, the stronger they would come, along with horrible anxiety. I stood in the kitchen crying and very afraid.

We got to church about twenty minutes early. We sat in the car in silence until other parishioners started to arrive. Madison sat in her car seat like an angel. As soon as we walked into the church, I started sobbing. Joey stood by my side and rubbed my back with one hand and held Madison in her carrier with the other. Everywhere I looked I saw a smiling face. Everyone gathered around to look at my beautiful baby. They commented on how perfect she was and how blessed we were to have such a wonderful gift. I stood there like a mannequin, crying, trying to muster up the strength to put a smile on my face. I kept looking down at the floor because I couldn't look anyone in the face. If I made eye contact, I knew they would see the pain in my eyes.

Hell on Earth

The hour-long mass felt as if it lasted five minutes. I cried the entire time. I felt the eyes of everyone around me staring, probably wondering what my problem was. Madison sat in her seat, smiling, and not a peep came from her little mouth. Then the priest made an announcement that he and the deacon would be giving healing prayers for the parishioners who needed them at the end of the mass.

I jumped all over that. I turned to Joey and said, "I'm staying! I need a healing prayer."

There were about three people ahead of me. I heard them praying for loved ones that either passed or had fallen ill. Then it was my turn. I was so nervous. A year and a half earlier, the same priest married Joey and me. Now I needed him to pray for me because I was losing my mind.

Father Bob was a loving, caring, friendly man. Deacon Pamela, his sidekick, didn't seem as friendly, but I didn't care; I needed their help. I walked up to the both of them, unable to speak. I couldn't control my tears. I don't remember my exact words, but when I was finally able to speak, I pointed to Madison sitting in her carrier and started to talk. "I'm a bad mother," I said. "I'm a bad mother, and a horrible person, and I don't deserve that beautiful baby girl over there. I don't deserve her. Please, can you help me?"

I knelt down in front of them, and they held my hands and prayed for me. Then something strange and unexpected happened. Deacon Pamela hugged me. She looked me in my eyes and said, "You're going to make it through this. I know you are. I went through the same thing myself, and it was horrible, but I pulled through, and you will too. You just have to have faith and a good support system. You will be fine."

I never would've guessed that the woman I assumed was unfriendly would share her story with me, but she did. I felt kind of bad because I completely misjudged her.

With that, they asked if Joey, Madison and I would join them in the rectory. I accepted and Joey followed my lead. Walking through the halls I recall the scent of burning palms and old books. Father Bob's office was open and not very well lit. He offered us some cookies and bottled water, which we graciously accepted, even though the thought of food made me nauseous. We sat with Father Bob and discussed pregnancy, birth and parenting. I told them about my whole nightmare birthing experience and how I was feeling. It was obvious that he wasn't truly familiar with my situation because he starting rambling on that I was mourning the loss of the fetus that I carried for nine months, and that soon I would be celebrating the life that was created. I was not relating to his story at all. I didn't understand what he was getting at, but he's a man, and I had to put that into consideration. I just smiled and agreed with him. I was happy to be in his presence; he was a man of God, and I could use all the help and prayers he had to offer. The next mass was about to start, so our little meeting had come to an end. We said "goodbye," and I promised that I would be back next week.

By the time we left the church, it was 12:00 p.m., and I didn't want to go home. There was a craft fair going on in the small town by the church. Joey is not a fan of heat or crowds, and it was 95 degrees with 100 percent humidity. Knowing this, I once again found myself asking my husband to do something he normally would never do. "Can we go walk around the craft fair?"

He nodded and we made our way in that direction. The streets and sidewalks were filled with people, and we were right smack in the middle of it all. I was going through the motions, looking in all the little booths, pretending to be interested. Then, out of nowhere, a new horrible thought started to torture me. I would get lost in the crowd and just run away, never looking back. Was that really what I wanted? Just to leave my husband and newborn baby and never come back. Absolutely not! But why was I thinking it? I loved my husband and baby so much; I would never leave them. The thoughts were just so foreign to my normal way of thinking, and it didn't make sense.

Joey and I took turns pushing Madison in the stroller. I was feeling guilty because it was so hot outside, and I had my three-week-old baby in the heat. Along with the guilt came the horrible thoughts and images of Madison getting sick and possibly dying because of my selfishness.

Through the crowds of happy people, I saw a familiar face. It was my Lamaze instructor, Lori. I hadn't seen or spoken to her since Madison's birth. At first I thought I was going to try and avoid her, but she recognized me right away. Lori is a very happy person, so full of life and energy. Normally, I was the same, but not anymore, and I knew it showed. My only saving grace was the sunglasses I was hiding behind. She walked right up to us and hugged both Joey and me. Then she turned to Madison and kissed her too.

That was the meeting that saved my life. Literally!

We chatted for a bit. Nothing involved, just small talk. Lori asked me how I was doing and I replied with "fine," and that was a lie. I was miserable. Lori was leaving the fair to go home. We said goodbye, and she walked away. Joey started to walk away, thinking I was behind him with the stroller. I just stood in the same spot, unable to move. I was thinking, not about the horrible scary thoughts I had become accustomed to, but that Lori was a Lamaze instructor and a registered nurse. She must know something about childbirth, and maybe she could shed some light on the way I was feeling.

When Joey turned around to talk to me, I wasn't there. As he started to walk back toward me, I said, "Watch the baby. I'll be right back."

I ran through the crowd, trying to catch up with Lori, hoping she hadn't left. I spotted her walking toward the parking lot. I grabbed her shoulder and said hysterically, "Lori, I'm not fine. I need help. There is something seriously wrong with me. I can't stop crying, and I can't make sense of my thoughts. I am so scared! Please tell me that you can help me."

She looked at me sincerely and said, "Wendy there is nothing wrong with you. You are going through so many changes, hormonal and chemical. I happen to know an excellent therapist, and I know you will really like her. Call me when you get home, and I will give you her number." Before moving toward her car, she gave me a kiss and a hug and promised me that I was going to be just fine.

As I looked back, Joey was standing there with the stroller staring at me. I ran to him and hugged him; I couldn't stop crying. I knew that I loved him and needed him. I was so afraid that he was going to leave me. I was apologizing to him and Madison. I didn't want to be this way; I hated myself, and I didn't understand what was happening. When I would have momentary bouts of sanity, I knew I was being totally irrational, but when I was in the throes of my anxiety attacks and obsessive-compulsive tirades, I wasn't rational.

It was so damn hot outside. I looked into Madison's stroller and saw that she was flush and sweaty. I started panicking again. *What if she passes out from the heat? Maybe she's dehydrated. She doesn't have all of her inoculations. What if she gets sick with something like the flu?* Now we were running through the crowd to go home. Besides, I wanted call Lori as soon as possible.

On our way home we called Radio Shack to check the status

of our computer. Surprisingly, our computer was ready to be picked up. There was nothing really wrong with it. It was a stupid software thing. I insisted that Joey pick it up and set it up as soon as we got home, and of course he agreed. He really is the best husband.

Once we got home, Joey placed Madison in her bassinet for a nap. I ran directly to the phone and called Lori while Joey set the computer up. Lori was waiting for my call, and that made me very happy. I went into detail about what I was going through and told her that I really needed her help. The therapist that she was referring to at the craft fair happened to be her sister, Irene, angel number two. Lori gave me Irene's number and said to call on Monday morning but told me that she would give her a call beforehand to get me an appointment as soon as possible. Lori gave me another telephone number—her friend, Sonia, angel number three, who was the Executive Director of the Postpartum Resource Center of New York. I sincerely thanked her, and she made me promise that I would call her in a few days to let her know how I was doing.

The cliché statement "everything happens for a reason" kept flooding my mind. I've said it a million times, never realizing its depth. In this situation, for me, it was so true. If I hadn't gone to that craft fair, I never would've walked into Lori. I truly believe that God put her there for me. It was a miracle; normally I would have steered clear from the entire situation. Joey hates large crowds, I hate the heat and we were not regular churchgoers. When I saw her, she was just about to leave. If I had gotten there one minute earlier (or later), our paths wouldn't have crossed. Seeing Lori saved my life; and I say "saved my life" because without the help of Irene and Sonia, I am not so sure I would still be here to tell this story.

At the time, my ambition to accomplish everyday tasks had disappeared. Cooking, cleaning, laundry and paying attention had become a fond memory. Joey had a pizza delivered to the house and forced me to eat a slice. On a normal day, I could eat about three slices. I love pizza, and who doesn't? Now I was forcing the pizza down my throat, trying not to gag.

Madison awoke from her nap, crying to be fed. Joey jumped right into action. He prepared the bottle and ran into the bedroom to feed her. I just sat on the couch like a zombie, staring at the wall. Joey sat on the couch right next to me and fed Madison. Just watching Joey feed her made me so anxious. I wanted to touch her, but it was as if something was holding me back.

I picked up the remote control and started going through all the channels. There was absolutely nothing on, or maybe in my crazed state I didn't have the attention span to notice. So the norm for me would be to put on some kind of news channel. I turned on one of the cable news channels, which coincidentally was broadcasting a story about a little girl who was kidnapped from her driveway and found murdered a day later at the hands of a neighbor. My stomach dropped, my heart started to race, and I began to panic. Who could do such a thing to a child, and why? Was I one of those people, and was that why I am having such crazy thoughts? I would watch the news at least three times a day, every day. Not anymore, no more news for me, not even the newspaper. As a matter of fact I stopped watching almost everything. Anything that had any kind of violence in it at all I just could not watch. I couldn't handle all the tragedies that came with a normal news broadcast. I would have thoughts of me being the star of a tragic news headline. I would get way too anxious, so I stuck with comedies and nonviolent cartoons.

I immediately changed the channel and put on Nickelodeon. It was a safe channel for me to watch. I told Joey that it was probably a good idea for us to get used to watching child-related television.

I don't know what I was thinking, being that Madison was only three weeks old, but Joey agreed with me. I guess he didn't want to disagree with anything I said for fear that I may have a nervous breakdown.

It was nighttime again, thank God! I was closer to Monday, and that meant I was closer to getting some help. I was actually looking forward to the next day. Then it dawned on me that Joey had to go to work the next morning. Oh my God! That meant he was leaving the house at 7:15 a.m. What was I going to do? *I can't be left alone. I'm crazy!*

I was right back into panic mode. I begged Joey to stay home from work, but he couldn't. He had already taken a week and a half off when I first gave birth to Madison.

Now what was I going to do? I had to call my mother. I knew she wouldn't say no. I just hoped that she hadn't fallen asleep yet. It was about 9:30 p.m., so it was a crap shoot. The phone rang about five times, and then the answering machine picked up. I went hysterical. "Mommy, are you there? Please pick up the phone. I need to talk to you. This is an emergency. Please call me back."

Within seconds she called back. I answered the phone crying like an infant. I don't even think I said "hello" when I answered the phone. "Joey has to go to work tomorrow morning, and you have to be at my house at 7:00 a.m. sharp because I cannot be left alone." My mother pleaded with me to calm down and promised me that she would be at my house by 7:00.

I went to bed another night with no physical contact with Madison. It was torture. I pleaded with God to help me and then cried myself to sleep.

Do You Plan on Hurting Yourself or Anyone Else?

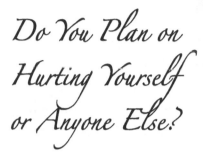

My eyes opened at 6:00 a.m. The alarm clock wouldn't go off for another half an hour. The anxiety and panic waited for me to wake up and planned their attack. I looked over at Joey, and he was fast asleep. I got out of bed and walked over to Madison's bassinet. She too was fast asleep. I stood there sobbing. She was so perfect. I rubbed her little face. She would pucker her lips together as if she were blowing kisses. It was so cute. I wanted to pick her up and hold her close to me, but I couldn't. I had horrible thoughts that wouldn't stop going through my head. Crying uncontrollably, I turned around and jumped back into bed. I took Joey's arm and wrapped it around me.

Then it hit me. Oh God! What if my mother forgets to come? Or, what if she wakes up late? What am I going to do? It was now 6:15 a.m. Was it too early to call my mother's house? I decided to wait to call my mom when Joey woke up and went into the shower. I had fifteen minutes left before that would occur. Another fifteen minutes to mentally torture myself. I just hung on to Joey for dear life. I was worried what the day would bring me, especially not having Joey there to support me. Everyone was safe when he was around.

The alarm clock went off at exactly 6:30 a.m. I didn't want to let go of Joey's arm. Thank God the alarm clock didn't wake Madison. Just as Joey went into the bathroom to take a shower, I picked up the phone to call my mother. I had to make sure she was awake or even better, on her way over. There was no answer. Which meant one of two things: she was still asleep or she was on her way.

I walked back into the bedroom and checked on Madison to make sure she was okay. She was still in a deep sleep. So I went and sat by the bathroom door, waiting for Joey to come out. I know it sounds crazy, but I was really afraid to be alone, and he gave me a very strong sense of security. I know that he was frustrated, but he knew that something was wrong because I never acted like that before.

My dog Petey started to bark, which meant my mother was at my door. I felt a bit of relief come over my body because she was fifteen minutes early to boot. I ran to the front door and threw my arms around her, as if I hadn't seen her in years. I was truly so happy to see her. With the hugs came the tears. I broke down and cried like a baby in my mother's arms. I had to regain my composure because Joey was coming out of the bathroom, and I didn't want him to see me so upset. I knew he was worried about leaving me as it was, and I didn't want to make the situation worse.

Joey gave me a big hug and a kiss goodbye. I could see the apprehension in his eyes. I knew he didn't want to leave me, but he had to. He had never seen me in this condition before. I just had this overwhelming feeling of impending doom. I said goodbye to him, holding back my tears. I had no idea what the day was going to bring me.

Would I actually make it through the day? Was I going to "snap" and act on my crazy thoughts? Was this the last time I was going to see my husband? One horrible doubtful question after the next flooded my head, but I had to pretend that I was okay so Joey could go to work with a somewhat clear conscience. I watched him walk to his car, wishing that I could go with him. I waved goodbye to him from the door, feeling like a lost puppy.

My mother forced me to get ready by starting the shower for me. I thought she was going to stay in the bathroom with me and wash me herself. I know she would have, but she couldn't because she had to get the baby fed and changed. I had a big day ahead of me, and I had to muster up the energy to get my ass in gear. I put on sweats and a T-shirt and threw my hair in a ponytail. I couldn't care less what I looked like. While I was getting ready, I picked up the phone and called Sonia and Irene. I left messages for both of them because it was only 7:30 a.m. I'm not sure what I was thinking. I guess I hoped someone would answer.

When I emerged from the bedroom, my mother had breakfast on the table waiting for me. It was my favorite: Count Chocula cereal. I really didn't want to eat it, but I knew if I didn't, my mother would tie me up and force feed me. My mother meant business; there was no joking around with her. I sat at the kitchen table staring at the bowl of cereal in front of me. My mother sat at the table right next to me, holding Madison in her arms, feeding her a bottle. I was so repulsed by the thought of eating. The cereal was sitting in the milk for so long that it turned into giant spongy pieces of mush. It was so gross, but I forced a few spoons of it down my throat just so I could say that I ate something. Every time I looked up, I saw the baby that I fed three days earlier in the same chair. I sobbed over my bowl of cereal.

My mom asked me if I wanted to help her change Madison, but I didn't want to. Physically I couldn't, I was paralyzed by fear. I wanted to wallow in my misery, so I sat at the table and continued to cry. My thoughts were going from one extreme to another, and they were all bad. Then I remembered something that happened about two years earlier that stuck in my mind. When Joey and I got married, we used a photographer with whom we had become friendly. His name was Ed, and his wife, Barbie, was his assistant. They were a very nice older couple who worked from their home. I recalled going to their house one day to pick up some finished portraits. When we arrived, we were greeted by several of their grandchildren running up and down the stairs. When we walked in, Barbie apologized for all the children and noise at the house. Joey and I didn't mind because we loved kids.

Barbie didn't look like her normal happy self. She had this extremely worried look on her face. She went on to tell us that her daughter, who had recently given birth, was just hospitalized. She had become extremely depressed and wouldn't leave the bedroom. I remember her saying, "She had too many children too close together, and now she's going through a really hard time." Ed and Barbie were helping out by taking care of the grandchildren while their daughter was in the hospital. Both Barbie and Ed looked exhausted. I felt horrible for them. At the time, I didn't understand what could bring their daughter to such an extreme, but I do now.

I went rummaging through all the paperwork I had from our wedding, trying to locate their phone number. It was only 8:00

a.m., but I didn't care, I was calling. What was the worst that could happen? Would she hang up on me? Would she tell me to mind my own business? Who knew? I was willing to take that chance.

The phone was ringing, and I realized that I had nothing planned out to say. How was I going to justify this phone call when someone picked up? I had to somehow explain myself in this hysterical state and hope to make sense. Luckily Barbie answered. I introduced myself and hoped that she remembered me, which she did. But why was I calling at 8:00 a.m.? I went through the whole story about her daughter and then I told her a little bit about what I was going through. I wanted to see if I could possibly speak to her daughter and maybe she would share her story with me. Barbie didn't seem too receptive to the idea. Her daughter had a very rough time and still had some issues she was dealing with. I asked Barbie if she would give her daughter my telephone number anyway. Who knew? Maybe she would call me. It was very discouraging to me to find that after two years she was still suffering. I apologized if I had overstepped my bounds and thanked Barbie for her time (P.S.—her daughter never called).

Now the wheels in my head were spinning. My OB's office didn't open for another hour and a half. I needed to talk to someone, anyone who would listen, but mostly someone who had some expertise in the medical profession. I knew that I was experiencing some kind of mental disturbance that I chalked up to sheer insanity caused by childbirth. I called my friend's mother, Joy, who was a registered nurse, and left her a message. I called my stepsister, Sunday, who had a baby about two years prior. She had become depressed during her pregnancy, so I left her a message too. Then I called my stepsister's mother, Carol, who was a retired nurse. She wasn't home either, so I left her a message. By that time, I felt defeated, so I plopped myself onto the couch and cried some more. My mother put Madison in her bouncy chair and sat beside me on the couch. I was like a baby again. My mother was actually cradling me in her arms. It probably looked really awkward, and my mom was probably uncomfortable, but I didn't care. I cried in her arms and couldn't stop.

Madison had fallen asleep in her chair. After I calmed myself down, I talked to my mom. It was so hard for me to put how I was feeling into words. I had never experienced a true bout of depression, so I didn't know how it should feel, but I surmised that was what I was going through. I had experienced plenty of anxiety and stress in my life, especially with my marriage and divorce with Neil, but I was able to cope and see the light at the end of the tunnel. The one thing I did know was that I wasn't getting better; I was getting much worse. I was feeling hopeless. I just kept telling her that I didn't want to be left alone, and I was really scared.

It was amazing how fast time went by with all my sobbing. Madison woke from her nap and was ready to take a bath. I wanted nothing to do with that, so I watched my mother do the job for me. I sat on the floor, looking into the tub. One thought after another was torturing me. *What if the water is too hot? What if it burns her skin?*

Images of her red burnt skin kept popping in and out of my head. Then new thoughts materialized. *What if she drowns? What if I drowned her? What if my mother drowns her?*

Images of her little lifeless body in the water were tormenting me.

I ran from the bathroom into my bedroom and jumped on my bed. I hid my head under the pillow trying, to stop the thoughts that were playing in my mind like a broken record. The more I tried to stop the thoughts, the stronger they were coming on. What was I going to do? I couldn't tell my mother what was going on in my head. She would have me put away. I tried to compose myself once again and walked back into the bathroom.

I was visibly upset, but my mother didn't ask what was wrong with me; she just continued tending to Madison. I followed my mother around the house like I was lost, from the bathroom into Madison's nursery. My mother was a natural so I just stood there, watching and sobbing. I was overwhelmed with guilt and anxiety. This was my job, not my mother's. I was totally incapable of caring for my daughter.

My mother had Madison on the changing table dressing her up. Above the changing table was a small mobile of a smiling sun. My mother pulled the string and the song that played was "Imagine," by John Lennon. Just then I broke down and actually fell to my knees. I was in such mental pain that I wanted to die. Out of the corner of my eye, I saw my mother and she was crying. Since that day, that song has a new meaning to me. Anytime I hear it now, it brings me back to that horrible place.

By now, it was about 12:30 p.m. I made another call to Irene and Sonia just in case they forgot to call me, and I also wanted to leave them my cell number. Right after that, we got ready and drove to the OB. The office had been open for about two hours already, but the doctor had just arrived. I told the receptionist that I didn't have an appointment but this was an emergency. I needed to see the doctor immediately. I literally walked right into the doctor's private office and sat in the chair with Madison on the floor in her carrier right in front of me. I wasn't leaving until I saw him. I was crazed. My mother thought I fell into a black hole; I just left her in the waiting room, wondering what was going on.

Dr. Jean is an older Japanese man. He is very tiny and absolutely adorable. I credit him with saving Madison's life when I was giving birth. If he hadn't been there, she wouldn't be here. Now I needed him to save my life.

I sat in the chair rocking back and forth with anxiety pumping my legs uncontrollably. Dr. Jean came and looked at me, then looked at the baby. I was just there about two weeks prior for my first checkup and everything was fine. Now I looked completely disturbed.

He sat at his desk and said, "Wendy, what is going on? You were so happy."

"Dr. Jean, I need your help. Something is really wrong with me. I can't stop crying. I feel horrible all the time. I don't want to be left alone, not even with the baby. Just look at her." I pointed to Madison on the floor. "She is perfect. I am a horrible mother. She deserves better. I feel like some kind of monster. Please help me," I sobbed.

The entire time I spoke, he sat across from me with a huge smile on his face. When I finished babbling he said, "You are fine. You are just going through a little postpartum thing. I see this kind of thing all the time. You are not that bad. I've seen a lot worse. Some of the women were so bad I had to send them to the hospital."

He seemed so nonchalant about the entire conversation, as if it happened all the time. Apparently it was very common, but he never mentioned it in the ten months prior to my delivery. He got up out of his chair and opened up a cabinet in his office and started going through all kinds of medication samples. I asked him if he was going to put me back on the birth control pill and told him what my friend Carrie told me.

He answered, "Nope! I'm going to give you this." It was a twenty-eight-day sample pack of Zoloft. All I knew about Zoloft was the commercial with the sad little rock with the black cloud over its head.

"But why not put me on the pill? It worked for my friend."

"I don't understand why her doctor prescribed her the pill. You haven't had your first menstrual cycle yet. I can't put you on the pill right now even if I wanted to. What you are suffering from is called postpartum depression. Start taking these pills tonight. Once a day. And I guarantee that you will start feeling better by the end of the week! I will call you in a few days to see how you are doing." He was still smiling . . .

Wow! Start taking these pills and by the end of the week I will feel better? That's amazing. He seemed extremely optimistic and was still smiling, so maybe he was onto something.

Okay! So I picked up Madison and wiped away my tears. My mother was climbing the walls in the waiting room. "What did he say?"

What did he say? "He didn't say much. He told me to take these pills, and by the end of the week, I will feel better. I don't think he knows what he's talking about, but what the hell!"

Postpartum Depression

It is estimated that 10-20 percent of new mothers experience postpartum depression; however, we suspect that this number is greater since many cases go unreported. Symptoms of postpartum depression are similar but more persistent (lasting throughout the day and longer than two weeks) than those of the baby blues. They usually develop a few weeks after delivery but can occur at any time during the first year after childbirth. Symptoms may include frequent crying, sleep disturbances, feelings of anger/irritability, suicidal thoughts, and sometimes anxiety or panic attacks. The new mom may feel overwhelmed, inadequate, and unable to cope.

Although exhausted, she is usually unable to sleep. She may worry obsessively about the baby's health, while feeling guilty about not bonding emotionally to her child. Many women are ashamed of their feelings and often do not seek help. Early recognition and proper treatment are important.

I started to drive back home. My mother sat in the backseat with Madison. Just then, my cell phone rang. The number didn't look familiar but I answered it anyway.

"Hello!"

"Hi! This is Irene. Is this Wendy?"

"Yes it is. Thank you so much for calling me back."

"Wendy I have to ask you this question. Do you plan on hurting yourself or anyone else?"

My heart dropped and I paused. Do I plan on hurting myself or anyone else? Nobody has ever asked me that question before. I didn't know what to say. By that time I decided it would be a good idea to pull the car over to the side of the road.

"Well, I don't *plan* on hurting myself or anyone else for that matter, but I don't know what's going on with me. I think I am going crazy."

"I have to ask you that. You don't have an actual plan to do anything. Do you?"

"No I do not. I just can't make sense out of what's going on in my head."

"Can you come see me tomorrow night at 9:00 p.m.? It's all that I have available now and I would really like to see you."

"Sure! I wish I could see you right now, but if I have to wait until tomorrow to see you, that's fine too."

"Okay. I will call you later on to give you directions. You are going to be all right. Just hang in there."

And that was it. She hung up, and for three minutes I felt sane. I was able to carry on a conversation without crying my eyes out. It was a goddamn miracle

I was back at home once again. I didn't want to be there, but there was nowhere else to go. Besides, it was so hot and humid that I wanted to get inside and feel the AC. I went straight into the kitchen trying to dodge all the horrible thoughts. I opened the sample box of Zoloft, which had 28 pills ranging from 25 milligrams to 50 milligrams. There were pamphlets in the box all about the medication. I read each and every one of them from front to back, spanning from depression to multiple anxiety disorders, including obsessive-compulsive disorder. Of course I focused on the bad stuff, dangerous side effects, bipolar disorder and suicide. Dr. Jean said to take the pills at night, but I needed relief, so I took it, even though it was only 2:00 p.m. Down the hatch it went.

My head was spinning. I missed my husband. I felt secure whenever he was around. He wouldn't be home for another two and a half hours. I needed to occupy my mind to try to distract myself from all the thoughts and confusion, so I decided to go on the computer to waste some time.

The computer was my best friend but also my worst enemy. I did a search on postpartum depression, and the first thing that came up was the story of Andrea Yates. On June 10, 2001, Andrea Yates had drowned her five children as a result of severe postpartum depression and psychosis. So, of course, I read on, focusing only on the postpartum psychosis.

Postpartum Psychosis

*Postpartum psychosis is a severe but extremely rare (1 or 2 women in 1,000) disorder that can develop in the postpartum period. This illness is characterized by a loss of contact with reality for extended periods of time. Symptoms usually occur during the first few weeks after delivery and include hallucinations, delusions, rapid mood swings, and suicidal/infanticidal thoughts or actions. Postpartum psychosis is a very serious emergency and requires **immediate** help. If you or someone you know may be experiencing postpartum psychosis, call your doctor or go to the nearest hospital emergency room.*

That was it, I was going psychotic, and I was one of the one or two in 1,000 women. I needed to go the hospital as soon as possible. I started to panic again. My heart was beating out of my chest, and my lips started to feel numb. I was having an anxiety attack. Time flies when you are torturing yourself.

The dog started barking, and Joey had just walked in the door from work. My mom was sitting on the couch in living room with Madison. I could hear them talking about me. Joey asked my mother how I was today and she replied, "Not very good. She cried most of the day." That was my cue to come in and tell them that I was psychotic.

I walked into the living room and sat on the couch, looking up at my mom and Joey. I said, "There is something wrong with me, and I need help. I was thinking that maybe I should go back to the hospital, and when I feel better I can come back home."

Joey and my mother were looking at me as if I had six heads.

Do You Plan on Hurting Yourself or Anyone Else?

My mother stood up straight with this concerned look on her face. She looked at Joey, then looked at me. "What do you mean you want to go to the hospital? Why?"

Joey interrupted, "If you think that I am taking you to the hospital . . . I'm not. You are going to be fine."

I started crying. "I hate the way I feel. This is not me. Maybe I am going psychotic, and I am losing control. I just want to go somewhere, anywhere, until I feel better. The best place for me to be is back at the hospital."

Joey and my mom looked totally baffled. Now my mother started to cry. Then Joey said "Wendy, If I take you to the hospital I am going to have to commit you. I am not committing you! I have committed people before. You would be with other people that are truly crazy. You are *not* crazy and you are *not* psychotic. I have seen and committed psychotic people. They see things that aren't there and hear voices. Are you seeing or hearing things?"

"No!" I said.

"Then you are not psychotic. You are going to be fine, and we are going to get through this. Did Irene call back?"

"Yes! I have an appointment scheduled for Tuesday night at 9:00 p.m.," I said.

"I spoke to some of the guys at work, and they told me that their wives went through a similar situation after their babies were born. They told me to have you call the PBA—Police Benevolent Association. They offer some kind of psychiatric program, and you can probably get in right away."

He got me the number, and I called. There was an answering service that I left my information with, and they would have someone get back to me as soon as possible.

My mom hung around and took care of Madison until Joey got

settled in. I just lay in my bed, crying. Just then, the phone rang, and it was the call I was waiting for all day.

"Hi Wendy, this is Sonia Murdock of The Postpartum Resource Center of New York. How are you feeling?"

"Not so good," I said.

"Wendy, do you plan on hurting yourself or anyone else?"

Wow, that was the second time in one day that I was asked that question.

"No! I don't plan on doing anything. I just feel like I am losing my mind. I don't know what's going to happen next," I replied.

"Wendy I want you to get a piece of paper and write these three sentences down: (1) I am not alone. (2) I am not to be blamed for what I am feeling. (3) I will be well and feel like myself. This is fully treatable."

At that point, I wasn't too sure that she knew what she was talking about. She had no idea what I was going through. I was never going to get better. I was going to be this miserable for the rest of my life.

I told Sonia about myself, the pregnancy, delivery and the series of events that brought me to that day. The only thing I didn't get into great detail about was the horrible thoughts I was having.

Sonia discussed the baby blues, postpartum depression and postpartum psychosis. Then she started talking about postpartum anxiety disorders. As she was describing the symptoms she said, "Mothers usually have thoughts of harm toward their baby and/or themselves and avoid the baby at any cost."

I interrupted and said, "What do you mean about thoughts of harm?"

"Well mothers will have thoughts of drowning their baby in the bath tub, smothering their babies with a pillow, stabbing the baby and other very violent thoughts. The thoughts cause extreme anxiety and fear of being alone."

Oh my God! That was me. I couldn't believe she said that.

"Sonia I have been having thoughts just like that. I was so afraid to say anything to anyone. I am scared to death. I don't want to be left alone for a second. Why is this happening to me? How could a mother have such crazy thoughts? I am petrified that I am going psychotic."

"You are not going psychotic," Sonia answered. "Repetitive, intrusive thoughts of harm to a child are hallmarks of postpartum obsessive-compulsive disorder."

Sonia then spoke to me about the Resource Center and her involvement. She went over the "Steps to Wellness," an extremely effective way to help women in a postpartum situation. The "steps" are education, sleep, nutrition, exercising, time for you, nonjudgmental sharing and emotional support. I literally wrote down everything she said.

Sonia went into detail on each and every step and then mentioned that the PRC—The Postpartum Research Center— offered "The Circle of Caring," which was a group of mothers going through the same thing I was going through. It met once a week. In addition, the PRC also offered telephone support from mothers that had already gone through postpartum depression and recovered.

I was on the phone with Sonia for about an hour. I was amazed at all the information that she provided. Before we ended the phone call, she told me that she was mailing me a packet filled with educational pamphlets, healthcare referrals, suggested reading, phone support telephone numbers and information regarding the Circle of Caring group. The downside for me was that particular group, unfortunately, wouldn't be starting for another month.

I didn't want the phone call to end. I finally made a connection with someone who was making sense to me. "Can I call you again tomorrow if I have any other questions?" I asked.

"Yes!"

Of course she said yes. I was on the verge of throwing myself into traffic. I am sure Sonia knew the last thing I wanted to hear was no.

After I hung up the telephone, I felt normal, but it was very short-lived. I started to doubt everything that Sonia had told me. How could she know if I was going to be okay? She didn't know me at all, but I had to have faith in something. I reread all of my notes from our conversation. Steps to wellness, hmm.

- No chocolate or caffeine. Chocolate was like crack to a crackhead for me. After that conversation, it was completely removed from my diet. No more Count Chocula for me. I never drank caffeinated drinks to begin with. CHECK!
- No alcohol, illicit drugs or cigarettes. That was never a problem. CHECK!
- Nutrition. Eat as healthy as possible. Lots of fruits and veggies. Get some Omega-3s incorporated into my diet. Go to store and get some supplements and fish, ASAP. CHECK!
- Spirituality. I already started going back to church and prayed all day long as it was. CHECK!
- Get as much vitamin D as possible. Sunlight helps increase mood. So I started standing outside practically staring at the sun. CHECK!
- Education. My goal was to get as educated as I possibly could. I would take it to a whole other level. Hello OCD. CHECK!
- Exercise. Within a day, I ordered several exercise DVDs and was

ready to get fit. CHECK!

- Sleep. That wasn't a problem because I had so much support from my husband and mother. CHECK!

Everything seemed to be in order. I could follow the Steps to Wellness, no problem, but would that do the trick?

I walked into my bedroom, and Joey was sitting on the bed, holding Madison. I felt my mood changing as every second went by. I couldn't sit still. Joey was staring at me and told me to sit down next to him on the bed. I sat right next to him and tried my hardest to relax. I actually lay down on the bed for about a minute, but quickly sat up. I felt like my skin was crawling; I was very anxious, and my mood was low. I needed relief; I just didn't know how to get it.

I wanted to get out of my house. Maybe I would take a ride in the car by myself. I needed to collect my thoughts. They were out of control. Then I asked myself, "Why do I want to go for a ride by myself? Would I come back? Does that mean I want to run away? Or maybe I want to drive my car off the road or into a tree. Then that would mean I wanted to kill myself. Did I want to kill myself?"

I was losing control. I took my hands and covered my face, trying to stop the crazy thoughts. Joey asked me if I was okay, and I wasn't. I was fighting a secret battle in my head.

"I think I want to go for a ride," I said

"Okay! I will get the baby ready," Joey replied.

"No! I think I want to go by myself."

"Okay. I guess that's a good idea."

I was frightened. I guess a part of me was hoping that Joey would say, "No, let me come with you," but he didn't. He was just going to let me leave. Was it meant to be for me to leave and possibly attempt suicide? I didn't want that, so I quickly jumped back into the bed and said, "Nevermind, I will just stay here."

The phone rang again. This time it was a therapist returning my call from the PBA. He didn't ask me if I planned on hurting myself or anyone else. He just asked a few questions about me and my situation and gave me an appointment for the following morning at 11:00. That seemed easy enough.

I spent the rest of the evening on the phone. Everyone that I called earlier in the day was calling me back, one after the other. I spoke with my stepsister, Sunny, who was depressed and medicated during her pregnancy.

"I am having a really hard time. I don't feel like myself at all. I am so anxious and I can't sit still. I went to my OB today and he started me on Zoloft. I am a wreck! Did you feel like this at all after your baby was born?" My voice started to crack as I was holding back my tears.

"I felt very anxious during my pregnancy," she replied. "But I went on antidepressants right away. After the baby was born, I was very emotional, but it was short-lived. The medication really helped me. Maybe you should talk to my mom. I know she was on Zoloft for a while, and it really helped her!"

Sunny's mother, Carol, was a retired registered nurse. I really wanted to talk to her because she was an educated medical professional. Hopefully she would be able to give me her expert opinion on my situation.

I went through my story from the beginning with her. Carol had come to visit me in the hospital when I delivered Madison, and I was my normal jovial self. Three weeks later I was a desperate, crying, emotional train wreck.

"Take the medication Wendy," Carol said enthusiastically. "It is a miracle drug! You will start feeling better right away. I never went through postpartum depression myself, but I have been depressed. Depression is depression. After taking my second pill, I started feeling better!"

That was exactly what I wanted to hear. Some optimism. I felt slightly better after talking with her.

Irene called back to give me directions. My friend's mother, Joy, another registered nurse, was extremely helpful as well. She informed me that her daughter-in-law, who I knew, suffered from PPD twice. She suggested that I call her. That helped, a lot. Finally, there was another mother that I could talk to and possibly relate to. By the time I got off the phone, it was 10:30 p.m. I had to prepare myself for another night of praying to God, then crying myself to sleep.

My eyes opened at 5:30 a.m. The anxiety, depression and horrible thoughts were still there. It would've been fantastic if this was all a horrible nightmare, and I woke and it was all gone. Unfortunately, I wasn't that lucky. It was just another shitty day.

My mom was at my house at 6:45 a.m., ready to start her newly appointed job. As my mother walked in, Joey walked out and was off to work. Madison was still sleeping, so my mother forced me to get in the shower before the baby woke up.

I cried in the shower for about fifteen minutes. When I walked out of the bathroom, my mother was sitting in the living room on a rocking chair, feeding Madison. She motioned for me to come to her. She stood up and handed the baby over to me and forced me to sit in the chair and feed her.

I stared at her beautiful little face. I wanted to be close to her. I wanted to be Madison's mommy again. I felt like an empty person.

I politely took his wife's business card and told him that I would call, even though I had no intention of calling her. I could only imagine what she was going to tell me. I was in awe when he told me that his wife was a social worker who specialized in women's issues. This guy didn't have a clue. I needed to hear him talk to me about the anxiety and depression that I was experiencing as a result of my pregnancy, not go off on a tangent about my childhood and the possibility that I was molested. I think he needed to communicate a little bit more with his wife. I wouldn't send my worst enemy to see him.

From that moment forward, my day was ruined. I didn't think that things could get any worse for me. I took two steps back. In this day and age, one would think a therapist would be a little bit more in tune to a hysterical woman who has just given birth to a baby, not to mention his wife specialized in women's issues. This man said everything that I didn't want to hear.

Before I left his office, I had to ask him if I should be hospitalized. "No, you do not need to be hospitalized," he replied. This, needless to say, did not make me feel better.

I couldn't control my emotions as I walked through the parking lot with my mother and Madison. I was crying and laughing at the same time. I felt so confused. I didn't know what to do with myself. I needed to hear a reassuring voice, so I called Irene. She was the only one, at that point, who could make me feel better. There was no answer, so I left her a message to call me on my cell phone.

It was only 11:45 a.m., and I did not want to go home. I needed to do something to occupy myself. My appointment with Irene wasn't until 9:00 p.m. So I decided to visit some friends from my old job at the car dealership. Maybe seeing them would spark something inside of me that would make me feel like my old self.

Do You Plan on Hurting Yourself or Anyone Else?

The second I walked through the door and saw all the smiling faces, I knew I had made a huge mistake. Everyone was so happy to see my beautiful little girl and me—she truly was beautiful. "Oh my God, she is gorgeous! Aren't you so excited? Isn't it amazing how much love you have for this little baby? Isn't being a mother the greatest thing in the world?"

I had no answers for any of those questions. I hated myself and everything about me. I knew that Madison was absolutely gorgeous. If it was about a week earlier, I could tell the world how much I loved her, but now I didn't feel a thing. I didn't know what to say, so I just nodded my head in an up-and-down motion and tried to put a smile on my face. I wanted to cry and did everything in my power not to. I tried not to look anyone in the eye. If they were to look in my eyes they could see the mess that I had become.

I knew I looked different physically. The last time most of these people had seen me, I was tipping the scale at about 200 pounds. Now, I was about 150 pounds, but I was not my normal, happy, cheerleader-self. I felt like everyone was wondering what was wrong. I kept trying to justify why I looked so shitty by saying I wasn't sleeping because the baby was up all night. I was lying.

After about ten minutes of torture, I had enough. I wanted to run out of the building and pull my hair from my head. I wanted to leave, but I had nowhere to go. At least when I was there I was not alone with my thoughts and anxiety. So I stayed for another half an hour.

Once again we were back in the car, and I was crying. I promised my friend Carrie that I would stop by and see her at work too. I worked with Carrie a few years earlier at another dealership, about five minutes away from this one.

I would, once again, put myself through more agony. Everyone was happy to see Madison and me. I forced smiles and laughter, pretending to be a doting mother. All the while, I was thinking of the meeting with that idiot therapist questioning me. Was I ever molested or raped? Did I block it out of my mind, and was it now resurfacing? My head was spinning in circles. I was hearing everyone around me, but I wasn't listening.

As I was leaving, there was a salesman that I knew outside smoking a cigarette. He came up to the car and said his hellos. Then he paused, looked at me and then Madison and said, "Are you okay? I know being a mother is hard work, but you will get through it. Keep in touch."

Did he know something? Out of all the people that I came in contact with that day, he was the only one who noticed that there was a problem. Not until I got better did I bring it up to him, and he did tell me he noticed that I was "different."

I left the dealership and cried to the sounds of "Mother's Little Helper" on the radio. My cell phone rang, and it was Irene. Like a voice from Heaven, I was so happy to hear from her. I told her about my crazy episode with the asshole therapist. She agreed that he was a bit off the beaten path. I told her that I couldn't wait to finally meet her. Nine o'clock couldn't come any faster.

The ride home was eternal. There was a great deal of traffic. Thank God my mother was there with me to try and distract me with conversation. I definitely did not want to be alone. I felt anxious, and all I did the whole trip home was think horrible thoughts. The thoughts ranged from me crashing my car into a tree to Madison falling out of the car. Needless to say, nothing happened, and we all made it home in one piece.

Joey was already home when I got there. I wanted to strangle him for suggesting that I see that horrible therapist. I was like a maniac trying to explain to him what happened. I was beginning to believe that I was molested, even though I wasn't.

There were several messages on my answering machine from friends and family wanting to say hello. For the most part, none of them knew what I was going through. At that point, I still wasn't sure myself. I had no desire, whatsoever, to return any of the calls. I didn't want to speak to anyone, which is very unusual for me. On a normal day, I would be on the phone for hours. As a matter of fact, I had no desire to do anything. My mood had plummeted to an all-time low. The only thing I was capable of accomplishing was crying.

I knew that I had to keep myself going until my 9:00 p.m. appointment. The other thing I knew was that my secret was going to be out. Both Joey and my mother were coming with me to see Irene, and I planned on spilling the beans, regardless of the outcome. It was important for me to make sure that I exposed everything that was going on with me. The only way I would know if I was truly a danger to myself or anyone else was if I told the absolute truth. I knew that my mother's love was unconditional, but was Joey's? Would he leave me? Would he think I was a horrible wife and mother? Was I going to be committed? Only time would tell.

I didn't take anything out to prepare for dinner, nor did I plan on cooking. Food wasn't even a thought for me. All Madison ate was formula, which should have made dinner easy for me to prepare for her. However, that was even a nightmare; as I prepared her bottle, horrible thoughts flew in and out of my head. My mind just kept going, and my stomach kept turning.

By 7:00 p.m., Joey was starving, so we took a ride to McDonald's. I forced myself to eat a hamburger. Since Friday, I barely ate, so a hamburger was a really big deal for me. We had a couple of hours left before my appointment, and I didn't want to go home, so we

I remember my mother commented to Irene that she had never seen me like this before, and she was truly worried. Her voice was cracking, and she too started to cry. She mentioned my wanting to go back to the hospital comment. I knew that statement alarmed both my mother and Joey.

"Wendy, why do you want to go to the hospital?" she asked.

"I am not sure. A part of me feels as though it would be a good idea. I would be safe there. More importantly I think everyone else would be better off. I need relief from my thoughts and anxiety, and maybe they could help me there," I said.

"Do you still want to go to the hospital now?"

Where else is there? What other options are there for a mother going through mental torture like this? At that point, I wished that I could go home with Irene. Honestly, if she told me I could go home with her, I would've.

"No I don't. I just need help. I am so afraid," I answered.

We were there for well over an hour. As the session was coming to an end, I grew extremely anxious. I didn't want to leave. Irene suggested that I see a colleague of hers, who was a psychiatrist. She even went as far as offering to call her and set up an appointment for me. I had never seen a psychiatrist before, and in my mind that was confirmation that I was completely insane, but I agreed. I needed help, and I was going to do whatever it took for me to get help and feel better. No matter what the cost. If Irene told me that smoking crack or shooting heroine was going to cure me, then I would've done it. We set up another appointment, and she told me I could call her at any time.

I couldn't believe the connection I had with Irene. She went above and beyond the call of duty for me. If she charged $1,000,000 an hour, it wasn't enough in my eyes. She was so sincere, and I felt that she really wanted to help. I wasn't just some other patient.

By the time we got out of Irene's office it was past 10:30 p.m. I said goodbye to my mom, making her promise me she would be at my house before 7:00 a.m. "Don't be late!"

The ride home was just bizarre. I just stared out the window, worried what Joey thought of the whole situation. I turned to him and asked him what was going through his head. He really didn't say much.

"You know that you are going to be okay. Right?" He said. I shook my head with approval and started to cry.

"Do you still love me? Are you going to leave me?"

"No, I'm not going to leave you, and yes I do love you. Now stop asking me."

There wasn't too much I could say to that. I knew in the past week that I had asked him that question several times, so I just turned my head and stared out the window again. Tomorrow was a new day of torture. I had no idea what to expect anymore. Sadly, I had nothing to look forward to.

Wednesday morning was here. Same shit, different day. My mother came on time, ready to work, forcing me to get up and get ready. What really sucked was getting up so early every day. I had the whole day ahead of me to feel like shit, and hate myself and everyone else.

What would be on the schedule for us today? If I was a normal, happy new mommy, maybe I would go to the beach, or go for a walk or maybe just stay home. I didn't want to do any of those things. The Wendy from a week ago wanted to go shopping for new baby clothes or spend hours taking pictures of Madison, but that Wendy was gone. I don't know where she went, but I desperately wanted her back.

walked by made me anxious. I felt so much guilt because I should have wanted to be in those stores buying all kinds of cute outfits and other baby bullshit. Now that was the last thing I wanted to do, and that made me feel horrible and guilty.

We entered Macy's, which was my mom's favorite store. She could spend hours in there. We went all the way up to the third floor via the elevator with the idea that we would work our way down. Plus that was where the baby clothing was.

My mother wandered off into the bedding section. I remember pushing the carriage toward the center of the store. I noticed some benches by the escalator that "had my name written on them." I just wanted to sit around, stare and not enjoy myself in peace. So I sat down on the bench pushing the carriage back and forth. Then I looked down the escalator and saw all the way down to the first floor. Just then, the thoughts and images flooded my head. What if I pushed Madison's carriage over the balcony down to the first floor? What if it was an accident? What if it wasn't? With the questions came the horrible images playing out in my mind.

I felt the salad I had eaten fifteen minutes earlier traveling back up my throat. I got really dizzy and sweaty. I stood up and pushed the carriage over to one of the cash registers thinking there would be a garbage pail or something to catch my vomit. Luckily there was but I didn't make it there in enough time. Thank God there was no one around to see me. I was so repulsed by my thoughts that it actually made me sick. I was devastated and wanted to leave ASAP. I found my mother within seconds of my puking incident and told her it was time to go. I made my mother drive, and I cried the whole way home.

I so desperately needed relief from myself. I hated this new life that I had and would do anything to change it. I felt so sorry for myself. I had been on the Zoloft for a few days with no visible results that I could see. I felt myself spiraling down into an even deeper state of despair. My thoughts were now beginning to focus not only on Madison, but on myself. Did I actually want to kill myself? The thought terrified me even though I tried to ignore it.

Was there a light at the end of the tunnel? It didn't seem so. When I got home I went to the mailbox and received the packet from Sonia, which I ripped into before I even got back into the house. As I walked in, the phone rang, and it was Dr. Abey, the psychiatrist; angel number four.

"Hello Wendy, this is Dr. Abey. Irene called and told me you needed some help. I have to ask if you plan on hurting yourself or anybody else."

There was that question again. "No, I don't think so," I answered.

Hell Week
Continues

*D*r. Abey scheduled my appointment for the next day, Thursday at 4:00 p.m. Although I answered Dr. Abey's question with a negative, I wasn't truly sure how I felt. I was hanging on by a string.

While my mother cared for Madison, I sat at the kitchen table and went through all the information Sonia had mailed to me. There was a phone support list of about six mothers who had experienced postpartum depression and lived in my area. I sat outside for vitamin D and started at the top, working my way down the list. I was on the phone for about three hours, speaking with all but one of the mothers. All of their stories were different, with varying degrees of severity. One had gone through psychosis, which scared me to death. She had been hospitalized several times and had attempted suicide. I was so anxious while

because both might involve thoughts about harming the newborn infant. Recently, a few serious cases of postpartum psychosis have received media attention, leading many people with pOCD to worry that they have psychosis.

In postpartum psychosis, the sufferer develops hallucinations (seeing or hearing things that aren't really there; e.g., "I saw smoke coming from the baby's ears") and delusions (strongly held beliefs that are not based in reality; e.g., "The baby is possessed by the devil and I must kill him to save his soul"). Postpartum psychosis is also an extremely rare condition, affecting 0.1 percent of new mothers. In some severe instances (but not in all cases), mothers with postpartum psychosis have actually harmed their infant, acting on their hallucination and delusions.

On the other hand, pOCD is not nearly as rare as postpartum psychosis, and pOCD is not associated with actually committing violence. Whereas a person with postpartum psychosis believes his or her hallucinations and delusions are true, pOCD sufferers are afraid of their obsessions and recognize that these thoughts and ideas are inconsistent with their worldview and general sense of morality. People with pOCD try to fight their obsessions. Finally, there is no evidence that pOCD symptoms can change into postpartum psychosis. These two conditions are very different problems.

What are the effects of pOCD?

- *Depression (sadness, loss of interest in people and activities, sleep loss or excessive sleepiness, loss of appetite, suicidal thinking, hopelessness, helplessness, lack of self-care).*
- *Problems with caring for the newborn because of fear and avoidance.*

- *Problems bonding with the newborn because of avoidance.*
- *Problems with one's relationship (marriage or partnership) because of extreme anxiety.*

Can pOCD be treated?

Yes, pOCD can be treated using the same methods used to treat other types of OCD. Strategies to treat pOCD include:

- *Cognitive-behavioral therapy (CBT).*
- *Learning that unwanted thoughts are normal and not dangerous.*
- *Challenging how the person interprets their obsessive thoughts.*
- *Gradually confronting situations and thoughts that have been avoided.*
- *Reducing the use of compulsive rituals to deal with obsessive anxiety.*

Selective serotonin reuptake inhibitor (SSRI) medicine.

- *Most medicines used to treat OCD are probably safe to use for pregnant and breastfeeding women, although it is important to check with your doctor about whether he or she thinks these medicines will be safe for you.*

How can I help a friend or family member with pOCD?

The first instinct of family and friends of people with pOCD is to tell them constantly that everything is going to be all right, and to do whatever they can to ease the person's anxiety. In the short run, this might put the person with pOCD at ease, but these types of "help" do not work over the long run. In fact, sometimes they make the problem worse! The best thing to do if a friend or family member is suffering, is to help them to arrange a consultation with a skilled mental health treatment provider, who can provide the right kinds of treatment for OCD/pOCD. Rather than trying to "force" them into getting help, it is best to talk to them about how things would improve if they sought professional help.[1]

I went to the pharmacy to fill my new prescriptions. I was a little embarrassed at the content of the prescriptions. Normally I would have prescriptions for antibiotics or allergy medication. Now I'm filing prescriptions for medications prescribed by a psychiatrist, and I had no idea what one was for. I waited forever for them to be filled. I was afraid that I might see someone I knew, and I didn't want to speak to anyone. I just wanted to go home and be miserable by myself.

Finally, after an hour, I was on my way home. Before I got to the car, I ripped the bag open and started reading the prescribing information. As I read about the Seroquel, I stopped dead in my footsteps: *SEROQUEL is indicated for the treatment of acute manic episodes associated with bipolar disorder and the treatment of schizophrenia.*

Holy shit! I am schizophrenic and bipolar. I felt my hands, lips and feet become numb. My heart was pounding out of my chest. I felt everything around me closing in. I was having a full-blown anxiety attack.

My mother got me in the car and tried to calm me down. Her advice was to call Dr. Abey as soon as I got home. I was freaking out. Once again I found myself in a state of sheer panic. I ran through the front door of my house in hysterics. Make way for the lunatic. I called Dr. Abey right away. I got an answering machine and left a frantic message.

1. Abramowitz, Jonathan. International OCD Foundation. 2009. http://www. ocfoundation.org/Facts.aspx

I immediately got on the computer and looked up Seroquel, schizophrenia and bipolar disorder. I was looking for signs and symptoms that I may have been experiencing. I was waiting for my mood to change or a new personality to come out as a result of my newfound illness.

Dr. Abey called back within minutes of my message. She explained that I was not schizophrenic or bipolar. Seroquel was indeed prescribed for those illnesses in large doses, but it was also used to treat other less serious mental illnesses in very small doses. I was taking a very small dose—the least possible. She prescribed it to calm me, control my anxiety and help me sleep until the Zoloft kicked in.

I guess I felt a bit of relief after her call, but I still doubted everything. There was a war going on in my head. My brain did not get a break; the battle was relentless. I took the tiny little pill that was cut in half and swallowed it. Hopefully this would do the trick.

It did something to me for sure. Within an hour the Seroquel kicked in, and I was a zombie. I couldn't function. I was completely numb. My head hit the pillow, and that was it for me.

Joey woke me up at 10:00 a.m. the following morning. My head felt like it weighed 100 pounds. I couldn't collect my thoughts at all. I was literally dumbfounded. I had a hard time articulating the simplest of words. This wasn't a good thing.

In addition to my lack of brainpower I had the worst case of cotton mouth. I wasn't hungry, but for the first time in a week, I was thirsty. I drank about a gallon of water in five minutes. According to the pharmacist, these were all normal side effects of the medications I was taking. And believe me, I was on the phone with the pharmacist twice a day.

Now, I was depressed, really quiet and gazing off into nowhere.

I think I may have even drooled on myself a couple of times. To add insult to injury, it was officially one week since my new life in Hell began. Nothing had changed, and I was even more depressed and anxious, but I put my faith in my doctor's hands and was in for the long haul. Something had to give; besides, this new medication was supposed to help with my anxiety until the other medication kicked in.

How long was this going to last? An even better question was, *am I going to live through this?*

My Friend OCD and Me

*O*bsessive-Compulsive Disorder (OCD) is a type of anxiety disorder in which you have unreasonable thoughts and fears (obsessions) that lead you to engage in repetitive behaviors (compulsions). With obsessive-compulsive disorder, you may realize that your obsessions aren't reasonable, and you may try to ignore them or stop them. But that only increases your distress and anxiety. Ultimately, you feel driven to perform compulsive acts in an effort to ease your distress.[1]

Obsessions as:
Recurrent and persistent thoughts, impulses, or images that are experienced, at some time during

1. Mayo Foundation for Medical Education and Research. 2010. http://www.mayoclinic.com/health/obsessive-compulsive-disorder/DS00189

the disturbance, as intrusive and inappropriate and that cause marked anxiety or distress. The thoughts, impulses, or images are not simply excessive worries about real-life problems. The person attempts to ignore or suppress such thoughts, impulses, or images, or to neutralize them with some other thought or action. The person recognizes that the obsessive thoughts, impulses, or images are a product of his or her own mind (not imposed from without as in thought insertion).

Compulsions:
Repetitive behaviors (e.g., hand washing, ordering, checking) or mental acts (e.g., praying, counting, repeating words silently) that the person feels driven to perform in response to an obsession, or according to rules that must be applied rigidly. The behaviors or mental acts are aimed at preventing or reducing distress or preventing some dreaded event or situation; however, these behaviors or mental acts either are not connected in a realistic way with what they are designed to neutralize or prevent or are clearly excessive. At some point during the course of the disorder, the person has recognized that the obsessions or compulsions are excessive or unreasonable.[1]

I used to think that people with OCD washed their hands a lot and were very neat. I never realized how much more was involved and never thought that I would be diagnosed with the same complex disorder. Looking back to when I was younger, I always had little quirks. I always worried about everything. As I got older, it just got worse, which I thought was normal. Everybody thought like I did,

2. Long, Philip W., M. D. Internet Mental Health. 2005. http://www.mentalhealth.com

and if they didn't, then maybe they just didn't care as much. It turns out that there are many facets of OCD. Not just hand washing and a need for order. I pretty much suffered from every single one.

Having gone through all this since I was young, one would think that I would've gotten some kind of help much sooner. I never saw anything wrong with my behavior. It made everyone else around me nuts, but I didn't care what they thought because to me it was normal.

I was always afraid. Afraid of what? Apparently everything. Through all of the years that I had suffered without ever understanding why, I started reading up on OCD and saw a medical professional who is a specialist; he truly educated me on the disorder. With all of my new knowledge, I compiled a list of all of the symptoms that I never realized were a part of a disorder. I just thought that I was weird, but here is a brief look into my friend OCD and all the time we have spent together over the years.

1. Illness

Since I was a little girl, I always feared that I was sick and dying. If I had a headache, I had a brain tumor. If I had a sore throat, it meant I had AIDS or throat cancer. I've had bone cancer, breast cancer, anthrax poisoning, heart attacks, strokes and several other terminal illnesses. You name it, I have had it. It made my family and friends nuts, they would tell me that I was a hypochondriac. And for some strange reason I am still alive and perfectly healthy.

I was convinced at one point in my life that mosquitoes could contract AIDS. So I tried to avoid being outside at any cost. If I did go outside, I was covered from head to toe and slathered in insect repellent, deet free, of course. I went to a concert with my best friend Stacy, and our then boyfriends. As we were driving to the concert, my hands started to go numb while I was holding the steering wheel. I was trying to ignore it, but then my feet and lips went numb. It was almost as if I was paralyzed, and I really started to panic. On our way to the concert, they took me to the hospital. I was convinced I was having a heart attack. After spending an hour at the hospital, they released me. Apparently I wasn't having a heart attack, and I felt much better. The doctor couldn't explain what was wrong. So we went on our merry way to the concert. About twenty minutes into the concert, it happened again. This time, I was wheeled out of the concert on a stretcher (very embarrassing) and taken back to the hospital in an ambulance. Once again, I was released. They had suggested that I have some tests run to figure out what was wrong. Oddly enough, it was nothing; nothing that could be diagnosed at the time. We missed the entire concert, and I ruined everyone's night.

Several years after that incident, I went out to dinner with my husband, Joey, and it happened again. As we were waiting to be seated I got this pain in my left arm and started to feel short of breath. Then the numbness came back to my hands, feet and face. I told Joe what I was feeling, and I started to panic. My husband rushed me to the hospital, thinking that I was having a heart attack. In a matter of seconds upon arrival, I had wires attached to me. They were performing an EKG and checking my vitals. In my mind, death was right around the corner. It turned out that I had a pinched nerve in my left arm and some really bad gas pains. The emergency room doctor told me that I was the healthiest person he has seen in a long time. I would find out a few years later that I was experiencing anxiety attacks. In addition, I also found out that OCD is an anxiety disorder.

Around the time of 9/11, I was petrified about everything. I was "one of those people" who walked around with a surgical mask on my face. I would get scared any time I would see a small plane in the air, with fears that they could be a crop duster spreading some kind of heinous killer disease. I would lock myself in my office at work and open my mail with rubber gloves on. I was convinced that somehow there was anthrax on my mail. I would start feeling flu-like symptoms or think I developed a rash and be at the doctor within hours. I had a full bottle of Cipro, just in case.

2. Medication

I never took medication. Who knows what could happen? What if it had some kind of adverse reaction on me and I died? There are people out there who take medication, even aspirin, then suddenly just drop dead. I couldn't take that risk because I didn't want to die. In the rare case that I would take medicine, it was rarely prescription. If I took aspirin or some kind of cold remedy, I would take half of the recommended dose and panic until about two hours after I took it. In that two hour span, I would be reading up on the medication, studying the side effects and adverse reactions. With all the stories on the news of people dying, going blind or deaf, I was too paranoid to take the chance.

For some reason the only medication I wasn't afraid of taking was stomach medication, and I don't know why. The only prescription medication I would take on a regular basis was my allergy medication. I would also get biweekly allergy shots and that's only because my mother would make me. My crazy medication rule even applied to Madison. I would have a very hard time giving her medication. I was so afraid that she was going to have a bad reaction to it. With that, I would give her half the recommended dose and watch her like a hawk for an hour in a state of panic. In my therapy sessions we would discuss my feelings about medication that wasn't as uncommon as I thought. Basically, it was my fear of the unknown and the minute possibility of something happening that would stop me from taking the medication.

3. AIDS

In my thirty-plus years on this earth, I can count my sexual partners on one hand, and I don't need all my fingers. I was still convinced somehow that I contracted it. After three tests, I am now convinced that I do not have the disease.

Once I was at a party and a fight broke out. After the fight, one of the men involved was bleeding. He didn't bleed on me, he bled near me. This particular person was extremely sexually active, and I was convinced he had some kind of disease, particularly AIDS. For the rest of the evening, all I could think of was contracting the disease, somehow. That following Monday, I scheduled an appointment to have an AIDS test; coincidentally, it came back negative.

4. Car accidents

I hold the people in my life very close to my heart. They are all extremely important to me. I would never want anything bad to happen to any of them. With that, I worried about all of them a great deal.

If there was a car accident, I would automatically worry that it was someone that I loved. Any time I was stuck in traffic the horrible images that would appear in my head drove me crazy. I would automatically start calling my friends and family from my cell phone to find their exact location. If I couldn't get through to them, I would go into a full-fledged panic attack. Half the time, it wasn't even a car accident causing the traffic jam. It was usually someone with a flat tire or some kind of pointless road construction.

I remember one incident when my parents had gone food shopping. About an hour after they left there was a horrible accident about a mile from our house. I begged my brother Michael to go to the scene to make sure it wasn't them. I was in a state of hysteria. After about twenty minutes of listening to me cry, my brother went to check it out. Guess what? It wasn't them, but I wasn't convinced because Michael didn't physically see the cars involved in the accident so I made him go back again. I needed physical proof, and to my happiness, it was not them.

5. Fear of loss

I was always afraid of losing someone close to me, usually by death. In my life I have been very lucky because I haven't experienced loss that close to me, with exception of my grandfather and my former sister-in-law's husband.

So far, my husband, mother, stepfather, siblings, best friends and close family have been involved in some kind of horrific accident (in my mind), and I have gone through many lengths to make sure that they are okay. So far, so good. For example, one winter there was a really bad snowstorm, and my brother Michael left at around 11:00 p.m. to go do some snow plowing for some extra money at the car dealership where he worked. Michael said he would be back in about an hour. I held on to his words. By 1:00 a.m. he wasn't home, and the panic started. I called the car dealership like thirty times, and no one answered. I even went as far as calling the 7-Eleven across the street, but no one spoke English, so they didn't understand what I was saying.

Now it was 2:30 a.m. I had these horrible images of him lying dead in the road. What if he was stuck in the snow? What if he got run over? I woke my mother and Vito, telling them that Michael wasn't

113

home. I was losing my mind. I wanted my parents to get up and go look for him. They yelled at me and told me to go back to sleep. Sleep? I couldn't sleep and couldn't believe their lack of concern for their son. I kept going into their room, screaming at the top of my lungs, but they kept throwing me out. I was totally outraged.

My brother Michael is about six feet three inches tall, 220 pounds, and was at the time, twenty-eight years old. He was more than capable of taking care of himself, not to mention that he was about two miles away from the house in a truck with a plow. I am aware of this now, but at the time, I couldn't control the way I felt; the horrible images and anxiety would just take over. I was so worried about him. I was ready to hop into my small rear-wheeled car and drive around in the blizzard to look for him. I was pacing the floor in my room losing my mind. Amazingly, my brother arrived at home around 3:30 a.m., safe and sound. I wiped my tears and wrapped my arms around him, as if he just came back from a war. I think he called me an idiot and pushed me into my bedroom, then told me to go to bed.

My best friend Stacy works in Manhattan. So naturally on 9/11, I pictured her dead or in some kind of danger. I remember being at work freaking out and crying hysterically. Yes, she did work in Manhattan, but nowhere near the Twin Towers. I called everyone; I would've called the mayor if I had his number. To make matters worse, all the phone lines were down. I had no control over the situation, and I was pissed. I just wanted to know that she was okay. At about noontime Stacy called me. She was fine, she happened to be stuck on a bridge when the planes hit the Twin Towers. She had received the hundreds of messages I left on her cell and home phones, so she knew she had to call me because if she didn't I would drive, walk or swim to get to her.

Worrying is what I do best, and I have worried a lot! If I could get paid for worrying I would be a millionaire.

6. And Everything Else

Quirky, strange and excessive are all pretty good words to describe how I behaved at times. For example, I collected pens. Not Mont Blanc's or Waterman's. Just pens! Ball point, felt tip, gel. It didn't matter. I didn't use them. They had to be in perfect working condition, with caps, if applicable, and in "out of the wrapper" condition. I still have a pen collection, but now I actually use the pens.

I used to take hour-long showers and washed my hands constantly. Touching doorknobs and handles made me nuts. And forget about going into public restrooms; I loathed them. When I was younger there, were no antibacterial hand sanitizers, so I was always washing my hands. I wouldn't touch things with my bare hands. I would use something, anything, as a barrier. Now I take normal showers that last ten-fifteen minutes, tops. I go in public restrooms and don't obsessively wash my hands.

I couldn't throw anything away. I found clothes from high school that I couldn't get rid of, and I didn't know why. It wasn't like I was ever going to wear them again. I just couldn't throw them away. I had even, somehow, lost a shoe and held onto the remaining shoe. The same rule applied to socks too. Broken pocketbooks, irreparable jewelry, belts from 1990, magazines, receipts from three years ago, old paid bills, empty makeup containers and perfume bottles, and any other completely useless items imaginable. I just couldn't throw them away. Maybe I thought somewhere down the line I would need them. Who knows? Now I have the ability to let go of all the junk, and Joey is thrilled. I actually went as far as having a garage sale to get rid of all my useless items. We finally have extra storage space.

Everything had its place, and my house was very organized. I separated *everything* into groups. For instance, all my lipsticks were in one container, all my lip liners in another, and my body lotion was separate from my hand lotions. I had an overabundance of everything, which gave me the ability to section things off. I had a collection of beauty products and perfumes that I never used. I don't know why I kept them. They were separate from the beauty products that I used on a regular basis. Now things are sort of organized and not separated in different containers. My overabundance of things no longer exists, and I use everything I have. With all the activity going on in my house, I have no time to be the clean freak from my previous life.

Invitations, Christmas cards, and thank you cards were a nightmare. If I was inviting ten people to a party I would have to go through twenty invitations. The penmanship had to be perfect. If not, I would throw it away and start over. Or sometimes I would be finished with the invites and reopen them because I was afraid that I put the wrong information in them, or that they weren't written out perfectly. Not so much anymore. I find myself throwing invitations together last minute, or just calling people and inviting them over the phone. Thank-you's are a memory of my past. I can't remember the last time I wrote out a thank you. Christmas cards are made up by the printer—no writing needed—and I don't care if eight-year-old Madison fills out the envelopes.

I was a perfectionist, and it affected everything in my life. Work especially. I started off going to college for accounting. I always loved numbers. While I was in school, I started selling cars. I stuck with that for about six years. Then I started working as a Finance Manager. More numbers. I was working with banks and crunching numbers to get the right payments and interest rates, I loved it.

My Friend OCD and Me

Somehow I became a Human Resources Manager for the same company. With that, I had to do payroll for about 400 people. Everything had to be perfect. I would spend hours in my office with the door locked, checking and double checking, and checking again. I was burning that midnight oil. Then I would go home and lose sleep just going through everything I did at work in my mind. Did I make any mistakes? Did I overpay/underpay anyone? Did I deposit the right amount of money into the payroll account? I couldn't sleep. Then I would go into work extra early before anyone got in to double-check once again. Suffice to say, I was very conscientious, and all my work got done correctly. With my new job as a mommy, I have no room for perfection.

I had a *very* big problem with being on time. I have never been punctual. I would get up really early, with every intention of being on time, but something always held me up. I was very fortunate to have the bosses that I had. They were very lenient with me because I was always late—except for payday. I guess they just accepted it.

I would wake up at 6:30 a.m., shower, and do my hair. I would do my hair over and over again, eventually putting it back in a ponytail. Dressing was another task. I would try on every outfit in my wardrobe, and nothing looked right. Ever! Every article was thrown about the room. I always wound up wearing the very first outfit I tried on. Go figure. I've even tried picking my outfits out the night before. That didn't work either. The next morning, I would hate the way it looked and wear something else. I have spent hours of wasted time.

After all that nonsense, it would be time for me to leave, and I was always running late. I would get into my car and drive to work, and halfway into my commute, I would start to panic. *Did I leave the curling iron on? Did I let the dog back in the house? Did I leave the windows open? Did I leave the iron on?* I would drive all the way back home to check everything. Even though I checked everything before I left the first time. Once again, I didn't know why. In certain instances when I absolutely could not go back home, I would beg my mother to go by my house to make sure it wasn't up in flames. Being the wonderful mother she is, she would go check for me.

At night before Joey and I would go to sleep, I would run around the house locking everything, checking the doors and windows, making sure the oven was off and there were no gas leaks. I would try to go to sleep, then get up and check everything again.

Nowadays, I am always on time. I can get ready in fifteen minutes. I have no time for picking out clothing. Everything I own is very versatile and comfortable. My hair takes me ten minutes tops. If it's raining or humid out, I just throw a baseball cap on. My checking rituals are also a thing of the past. I check once and I am done.

Possibly saying the wrong thing and offending someone or hurting his or her feelings would send me into an anxiety attack. I would lose sleep at night worrying and preparing my conversation with that person whom I may have offended. When I was younger, I was very insecure about my relationships, not to mention myself. I cared too much about how other people perceived me. I was horribly insecure. I always tried to be a crowd-pleaser. If I had something that someone else wanted, I would give it to them. It didn't matter what it was. I pride myself on being generous. I was everybody's friend and wanted everyone to be my friend. I would get so upset if I thought someone didn't like me. I would take it so personally. I'd sacrifice my happiness to make other people happy. In some cases, people would walk all over me because I was a big pushover.

I am no longer a pushover, and I could not care less what anybody thinks of me with the exception of my close friends and family. Now, if I offend someone, it's probably because they deserve it. If someone doesn't like me, I will not lose sleep. I am still very generous and would give you the shirt off my back. My new appreciation for life has categorized material things as just "stuff" that can be replaced.

These other items on my OCD list are a work in progress and not too bad, or require therapy (in my opinion): I could not walk barefoot on grass. If the grass was wet, I would avoid it at any cost, even if I was wearing shoes. I got completely grossed out by it. I am still having issues with the grass thing, but I am working on it.

I would consider myself a pretty religious person. I didn't go to church regularly, but I did pray every night. I believed very strongly that you would be punished for your sins, so I always tried to do the right thing. I believe in God and the Devil, and I definitely don't want to go to Hell when I die. In the past, I would worry sometimes that I would forget to pray for someone. By doing that, somehow, it would affect that person in a negative way and make something bad happen. So I would start my prayer ritual all over again, going through the list of people I want to pray for until I got it right. I still pray, but now it is okay if I forget to mention someone because I realize that nothing is going to happen.

I was and still am a news fanatic. I have been watching the news since I was about six years old. There is a 24-hour news radio station on in my car every time I am driving. I have to know what is going on at all times. That is one thing I guess needs a bit more work/therapy.

Jagged, unkempt finger and toenails can send me into a fit, especially if I put my fingers through my hair, and a strand gets caught in my nail. Or if my toenails get snagged on a sock or a blanket, I completely freak out. I need a nail file immediately. If I don't have one, I get extremely anxious until I find one. I will wrap my finger in tape or try to cover it until I find relief.

I have to sleep in a neatly made bed, and I refuse to sleep in an unmade bed. The sheets have to be tucked in tight, and my feet have to be covered. I sleep like a dead person, so when I wake up the bed is pretty much made. My husband on the other hand, sleeps like he's wrestling someone. He is all over the bed. His side of the bed is a mess. The pillows end up on the floor, and the sheets are pulled out. It makes me nuts. I don't know what he does at night. I will wake up and fix the bed in the middle of the night or go sleep on the couch.

I smell everything. I know that sounds gross, but I can't help myself. Whether its food, books, paper, magazines, clothing, you name it, I smell it. There are certain smells that make me sick. I don't mind garlic while it's being cooked, or the taste of it. What I do hate is the smell of garlic on someone's breath. No matter what anyone does to mask the smell of garlic on their breath, it does not work. Not only can you smell it on one's breath, it emanates out of their nostrils and pores, and it drives me bonkers. It can stink up an entire room. I try my hardest to avoid garlic any way possible.

The smell of dog poop makes me sick, too. I can smell it from miles away. It's funny because I have four dogs, two of which are German Shepherds that take huge poops. I make Joe go on "poop patrol" once a day.

I have to pick at pimples or any imperfections on my husband's or my skin. I have a special little tool that I use to extract all the nasty junk that comes out of the pimples. It makes my husband crazy, but I can't control myself. It especially bothers him when I do it in public, or when he is driving. So I have to restrain myself until I get home. When it comes to me, I will pick and pick until I bleed (I know that sounds really gross). I walk around with huge welts on my face.

I watch movies over and over again, especially if I really like them. The same thing goes with songs; I can listen to a song 100 times in a row.

I need a very clean windshield. Any sign of debris or water, and I freak out; I have to clean it at once. I carry window wipes in my car, just in case I run out of washer fluid. Even if I am not driving, I request that the windshield be cleaned off. I can't stand it when it starts to rain, and the driver doesn't put the wipers on. I am not even sure if that's OCD, but it's very irritating and I know it.

Over and over again. That's how things play in my mind. Whether it's music, conversations, sounds, or images, they play in my mind like a broken record.

If I am collecting something, no matter what it is, I have to have the complete collection. Missing pieces make me crazy. If I am missing a piece to something and I cannot replace it, I will throw it out or give it away. Like silverware or game pieces. The same thing goes with any crafts or projects I start. If I am painting, I have to have every tool needed. All different brushes and finishes. I am like Salvatore Dali. Scrapbooking is one of my weaknesses. I have every scrapbooking tool on the market, but I rarely use them.

I know the basics about haircutting and cosmetology. I am not a licensed beautician, but I own haircutting scissors, trimmers, hair coloring bowls and brushes, waxing kits, etc. I could probably open my own salon with all the products I have.

I like things to be in new condition. Like books and magazines, sometimes boxes and shopping bags. The pages have to be perfect; no creases or rips. If they are defected in any way, they are garbage to me. It makes me crazy when people turn pages and wrinkle the paper, and that goes with any kind of paper. If it's wrinkled it is garbage.

After Madison fell asleep, I buried my head in the books I had gotten from the library. I needed to do something to occupy my brain.

My days were eternal, just waiting to feel better. I was spending most of my time reading books and researching PPD and OCD. It was so discouraging. Both Joey and my mom tried to keep every day active for me. The medication was numbing me, and to make matters worse, I still felt anxious, depressed and extremely detached from everything.

In one of the books I read, it suggested that I pick a time during the day to cry and let out all of the pain. One of the suggestions was to do it in the bathroom while I showered. I had started doing that from the beginning, only now I would actually take a shower, not stand next to it and cry. So that became a daily ritual for me. I would stand or sometimes sit in the shower and sob. It was a pathetic act, but I tried anything that would work.

During the day, my mother would plan trips for us to the beach or the park. I would force myself to feed and sometimes change Madison. Although it caused me terrible anxiety, I had to do it. By the third week of suffering, I had a library of books to read. I must have had fifteen books on mental illness, hormones and postpartum depression. I would read passages pertaining to my condition over and over again, even highlighting and taking notes on important facts. It was like I was studying for an exam. It was a test for my life.

One of the worst things I did to hinder my recovery was compare myself to other people and set deadlines for myself. My thirtieth birthday was August twenty-ninth. My goal was to feel better by that day. Well, needless to say, I did not get better by then. My family wanted to throw a big party to celebrate the occasion, but I wanted nothing to do with it. As the day neared, I realized that I wasn't getting better, and that made me spiral into an even worse depression.

Irene told me that she was going to be in California the week of my thirtieth birthday. Even though Irene was all the way at the other end of the country vacationing with her family, she still found the time to call me several times while she was away. I was thankful for that; I don't know how I could've made it through that week without hearing her voice. She had suggested that I set no time limit for my recovery, and she was right. Irene predicted that I would be disappointed, and I was.

The week of my birthday, my whole family did everything they could to make me happy. I knew how hard everyone was trying, and it made me feel so guilty. My husband bought me beautiful jewelry and took me out to really nice restaurants. My mother got me a full day of beauty at a spa, and a ridiculously overpriced diaper bag. The gifts were endless and beautiful, but they didn't mean anything to me. I could've won the lottery for a billion dollars and it wouldn't have made a difference in my life. No amount of money could buy what I wanted.

My friends wanted to take me out for my birthday the following weekend to celebrate this special milestone. The big three-O! I was so petrified to go out, but I had to do it. If not to do it for my friends, I should also do it for myself. Their hearts were in the right place, and I loved them for that.

My friend Kerri made reservations at a really nice restaurant, and Stacy and her husband were going to meet us there. Our reservations were set for 8:00 p.m. I had to mentally prepare myself for the outing all day. Joey was staying home to watch Madison so I could go out.

Normally going out with my friends was a favorite pastime. We would go to bars or clubs and have a blast, staying out until all hours of the night. The last time that I had been out drinking with my friends was in September of 2001, which was right before I became pregnant. After the nine months of pregnancy, the added seventy pounds of fat on my body, the 100 degree heat and the grueling labor, I wanted to go out and have a good time. I told Stacy and Kerri to get ready for my thirtieth birthday two months in advance. I wanted a big party, limousines and a hangover. Well, now the time was here, and I didn't want to do anything. For the first time in my life, I wanted to be alone, feeling miserable. I couldn't give into the depression. Even though this new Wendy didn't want to go, the old Wendy made her do it. I had to do it.

Not that I am an alcoholic, but when I go out with my friends, I like to let loose and have a couple of drinks. Now the option of having any drinks at all was not in the equation. I was severely depressed and on medications that specifically says *not* to drink when taking them. Drinking alcohol on the meds could send me spiraling into an even worse depression, and for me, there was nowhere else to go. They didn't ask any questions; Stacy knew what was going on with me and I had recently told Kerri as well. They were just happy that I came out that night.

The whole day I worried. I wanted to go out and have a good time, but my heart knew I wasn't going to. Kerri came to get me at about 7:30 p.m. I tried to make believe I was really happy and ready to have a good time. We chatted the whole way to the restaurant, but in the back of my mind, all I could think of was Madison and the horrible reality that was my life.

We got to the restaurant, and Stacy and John were already there waiting at the bar. I felt like I was in another world. I put a smile on my face and did the best I could to seem normal. Not to mention the medication I was on made me really lethargic and loopy.

We talked and laughed. I opened my gifts and over-exaggerated my reactions. The gifts were very nice, but I really overdid it. I just felt so disconnected from the world. I was there, but I wasn't. I wasn't sure how I was supposed to feel. Should I be happy because I wasn't home? Should I be missing Madison because I was away from her for the first time? Should I miss Joey? Was I even having a good time? Could everyone I was with tell how horribly depressed I was? I felt like complete shit.

The meal was delicious. I couldn't believe that I actually ate. They surprised me with a cake, and the restaurant staff came over and sang "Happy Birthday" to me. Then it was time to make a wish. I tried my hardest not to cry, but the tears were jumping out of my eyeballs, and my lips began to tremble. I wished that I would get better. Even just a little bit better would be great. All eyes were on me, and it was really awkward, but I didn't care anymore. They were my best friends, and even though they couldn't relate, I knew that they realized how unhappy I was. This was not the "Wendy" that everyone knew.

As the night came to an end, I was happy that I went. I would've been disappointed in myself if I didn't. We all said goodbye in the parking lot, and my obsessive-compulsive thoughts came back. *What if I never saw them again? What if I killed myself from this crushing depression? Did I want to kill myself? What would my friends think of me? Would they hate me for it? Would they even care?* I tried to stop the thoughts, but they were unrelenting. I kept saying to myself, *"That is absolutely ridiculous. Why are you thinking these things?"* But it didn't help or stop anything.

When I arrived home that evening, it was as if I never left. Everything was the same. My dog Petey greeted me at the door. Joey had Madison on his chest, and they were both fast asleep on the couch. I picked up Petey and carried him around the house with me, looking in every room. Joey had cleaned the house and did the laundry. Life was going on without me. I was so alone and isolated. This was my house, and I felt like a stranger to my family. I sat on the floor with Petey in my arms and cried uncontrollably. Petey was just looking at me, letting me cry all over him. I wanted to die.

I became a ghost. I spent my days with my mother, Madison and Joey. From time to time, I would speak to my friends and lie, telling them I was feeling better. I spent a lot of time talking with my phone support and therapist—Ilene and Irene, respectively. I couldn't wait for the Circle of Caring group at the PRC to start, but that wouldn't be for another few weeks.

On Joey's days off from work, we would take rides out to the east end of Long Island. It was so peaceful. It was so much better than hanging out in my house, looking at the same four walls and waiting to get better. We would walk around the quaint little villages and window-shop, but I was still a robot. The medication was working, I guess. I was feeling a tiny bit better because I was able to eat. That was something that Joey noticed as well. I needed to stay positive and optimistic with hopes that my mood would improve that much more.

By the middle of September, I had lost all of the baby weight and then some. I went from 210 pounds to 135 pounds in about two months. Some would say that depression is the best diet there is. I would've rather kept the weight on than feel the way I did. I was aware that my mood was progressing, but I still had a long road ahead of me. The tormenting thoughts and anxiety were still there, but I needed the depression to lift a bit more before I could work on everything else.

I barely talked anymore. On our many rides around Long

Island, I would just stare out the window. Joey said that he enjoyed the quietness while it lasted (I guess that meant I spoke a lot), but I didn't believe him. Joking around and having a good time with Joey was something that people admired about our relationship. We never took life seriously and always communicated with each other. I think I used to be fun and witty. Now, fun wasn't in my vocabulary, and witty wasn't something I would use to describe myself.

I was caring for Madison a bit more, but I wasn't feeling any emotion. I still couldn't be alone. I had 24-hour surveillance, and it didn't bother me one bit. The thoughts of harm were still there and going strong along with the anxiety. But now the focus was on me. If the thoughts that were popping into my head involved anything bad happening to Madison, I would move the focus onto me. The one thing I knew for certain was before I would ever harm Madison, I would harm myself.

Joey had been in law enforcement since August of 1999. It never dawned on me that he carried a gun, and it was kept in a safe five feet away from our bed. Well, I knew that he had one, but I never really thought about it. As my thoughts often changed direction, I thought about shooting myself a lot. I was petrified. I knew that I didn't want to shoot myself, but the thoughts were there, and that made it a reality. I made sure that every day when Joey came home from work, the first thing he did when he walked through that door was put his service revolver right in the safe. It got to the point where I wouldn't even walk near the safe. I would actually jump over the bed to avoid going near it. I couldn't even look at the safe without having an anxiety attack.

The thoughts of harming myself became so bad that I couldn't shave my legs anymore. One day I was in the shower, and I began to shave my legs. I noticed the little thin blades on the razor head.

Thoughts started to flood my head that I could slit my wrists and bleed to death in the shower. Was it what I wanted to do? Absolutely not, but once again the thought was there. I threw the razor into garbage and away from my sight. I was just so frustrated that I felt as bad as I did. I wanted to be me again; I felt so lost.

My new conflict was how to shave my legs. At the time, I didn't have any depilatories or wax, so I grabbed Joey's electric razor and tried to shave my legs with it. Needless to say, it did not work at all. So from that day until I got better, I used hot wax to get rid of the hair on my legs and a depilatory for the hair under my arms.

One day, my mother and Vito thought it would be a good idea to take me and Madison to the aquarium. It sounded like a good plan at first, but it didn't end up that way. When we walked through the doors of the aquarium, it was packed with people. I wanted to leave the second we got there. It was almost impossible to walk around, not to mention Madison's huge stroller. I think you need a license to navigate one of those things. I was extremely anxious and agitated.

As we walked toward the center of the aquarium, I noticed this tremendous shark tank, and it was feeding time. I started to sweat, and my hands became numb. They were throwing clumps of a bloody, fleshy mess into the water. I automatically had images of Madison's little body being thrown into the tank. Then the images changed, and it was my body being eaten by the sharks. Then came the "what-ifs." What if Madison fell into the tank? What if I dropped her in there? What if I jumped into the tank in a sad suicide attempt? I was actually hitting myself in the head trying to stop the thoughts and images. After fifteen minutes being at the aquarium, it was time to go. I felt really bad for my parents, but I couldn't take it anymore.

I think I had a nervous breakdown that day. For the first time, I truly feared that I was going to commit suicide. I felt really out of control. My mother came to my house with me and tried to calm me down. I called Dr. Abey and left her a frantic message that I needed to speak with her. I also called Ilene sobbing to her on the phone that I was feeling helpless and out of control. I was truly scared for myself. I didn't think I was going to make it through this time. I really have to give her a lot of credit because she did her best to calm me down, and it worked. Ilene brought me back to her PPD experience and really sympathized with me. Her ability to familiarize with me and discuss her recovery gave me hope.

Dr. Abey called back and was very concerned about me. By the time she had called back, I had already calmed down a bit. I told her that I was feeling very out of control. She suggested that I go on a mood stabilizer. Something had to give, because I was hanging on by a string. She called in the prescription to the pharmacy, but I never picked it up.

I started screwing up my medication doses. My mind was so gone that I had no recollection of when I took my medication. I called the pharmacist in a panic that I possibly overdosed on my meds. I had convinced myself that I had taken my medication twice in one day. The pharmacist spoke to me like I was six years old. He reassured me that if I had actually taken an additional dose of the medication that nothing would happen to me. *If* I did take an extra dose, I could possibly feel a little tired, and that was it.

I was convincing myself that the overdosage would cause some kind of strain on my brain, causing me to "snap" and go insane. After an hour or so went by, I realized that nothing was going to happen, so I went on with my miserable day.

In my sessions with Irene and Dr. Abey, I made sure that I told them everything that was going through my head. I assured them that I didn't want to kill or harm myself, but once again, my thoughts were telling me to. That was the OCD's way of rearing its ugly head. I put way too much merit in my thoughts, and sometimes I was not able rationalize their graphic nature. I had to keep in mind that a thought was just a thought. The depression made it very difficult to see things on the bright side. Thinking back to some rough patches in my life, the thought was there, but I was able to dismiss it because it was just so ridiculous. I was having such a hard time now, and I am sure that other people who don't suffer from anxiety disorders, namely OCD, would think that I truly needed to be checked into a mental hospital. I never wanted to kill myself, which was why I suffered such anxiety. If I wanted to end my life, I would've just done it with no remorse.

I started to feel very responsible for the way I was feeling. Maybe I wasn't as good a person as I thought I was. Maybe I was being punished and deserved this hell. Or maybe it was time to right some wrongs in my life, and I needed to do some soul-searching. Maybe there was something that was missing in my life that I was longing for. And maybe that missing link was crucial to my recovery. I was so determined to get better that I would do whatever it took.

In the middle of all of this soul-searching, I had developed a really painful ingrown toenail. It hurt so bad that I couldn't wear shoes. This too was a part of my punishment. Joey said that he knew how to fix it, so stupid me, I let him go to town on my toe. Dr. Joe used a toenail clipper and a razor blade. I had no idea what he was doing. It felt like he was removing my whole toe from my foot. The pain was excruciating, and I was bleeding all over the bed. But this pain was well deserved; it was part of my retribution. After an hour went by, I couldn't take the pain anymore; besides, I may have needed a blood transfusion from the loss of blood. Luckily, I found a podiatrist who would take me in immediately. He used numbing agents and sterile tools to repair the damage my loving husband did to my poor little toe. I will never do that again. Lesson learned!

The next day, I was at a park with my mother and Madison, and we got to talking. I told her that I somehow felt responsible for what was happening to me. I was trying to find that missing link or I needed to apologize for something that I had possibly done wrong. Of course she told me that was crazy. I needed to close all the open doors in my life and have peace in my heart.

Then it crossed my mind that I hadn't spoken to the sperm donor, my biological father in over a year. We had a very strange relationship due to his unconventional lifestyle. He really wasn't much of a father figure; he was more of a long lost friend than anything else. Everyone else was more important to him than his own children. On the outside he is extremely likable and is very charismatic and has a way with people. Everyone that meets him immediately likes him until they get to know him. What kind of man abandons his children? It's one thing to be unfaithful to your partner, but it's a whole other issue when you walk away from your own children. The sperm donor had three biological children that he had walked away from to better his own life. He had a very turbulent relationship with my brother Michael. During the infamous phone call from the sperm donor when he backed out of any responsibility for my first wedding, it was Michael who grabbed the phone and came to my defense. Their relationship never recovered after that day. Once someone crosses Michael in the wrong way, they're done. Michael is not very forgiving. As for me, I am a bit of a pushover and forgive too easily. I did love him; after all, he was my biological father, and I was powerless to change that. I decided that I needed to contact him. He had no idea that I was even pregnant, let alone that I had given birth to his one and only grandchild. I knew that he

him. I made up some crazy story that I walked into him at the bank. Eventually I told him the truth because he wasn't buying my story. I wasn't sure what his reaction would be. Joey had met the sperm donor several times since we had dated. He thought he was a nice guy, just not a very good father.

Joey's reaction was very neutral. If it was something that would make me happy, then he didn't care. Knowing how vulnerable I was at that time, he just didn't want to see me get hurt. He did say that he felt it was too early to have a big family get-together with him, but we went that same night anyway. Joey did whatever it took to help me get better!

We showed up at the sperm donor's house after dinner and met his new family. Everybody was very gracious and seemed happy to meet us. The sperm donor's new wife, Carolyn, was very sweet but seemed a little taken back by the visit. As far as she was concerned, I was a horrible daughter. After a few visits, Carolyn questioned me about my relationship with the sperm donor. The sperm donor told her that the reason we were estranged was because I refused to see my grandmother (his mother) when she was in the hospital and then refused to go to her funeral when she passed away because I hated his family. The real version went something like this: his family was never very fond of me because I always favored my mother's family. Reason being: they were involved in my life and showed interest in everything I did. The sperm donor's family couldn't care less about my brother or me. They were never involved in our lives when my mother was married to the sperm donor. I didn't go to the hospital because 1. I had no idea she was even sick, and 2. I was seventeen years old and didn't even have a car to drive to the hospital, assuming I even knew she was there. As for the funeral, I didn't find out that she passed until three days after she was buried. My stepfather, who

144

found out through a mutual friend, was the one who told me. His friend wasn't sure when she died but knew where the funeral home was. Vito took me to the funeral home only to find out that I missed the funeral by a few days.

I was shocked that the sperm donor admitted that he lied about the whole situation. My stepmother made the sperm donor promise that he would fix the entire mess that he created, which he never did.

It was nice having the sperm donor and his family involved in my life while it lasted. I guess it was kind of a distraction from everything else that was going on but it wasn't the magic fix that I banked on.

Andrea

*A*s the days went on, I became more and more confused and angry. I still didn't believe that I was going to recover from this. I thought that my doctors and caregivers were misdiagnosing me. I wasn't convinced that this was only postpartum depression. I truly believed that I was suffering from postpartum psychosis or schizophrenia. I was just waiting to snap or lose control.

How could I be having these crazy images of harm to my beautiful baby and thoughts of suicide and not be a danger? I was telling my psychiatrist, therapist and an expert on PPD about what was going on in my head, and no one seemed alarmed. I just didn't get it. This is how every horrible news story is created. I could see the headline; "Woman Goes Psycho and Kills Family, Then Herself."

I needed to do some research myself to try and stop the impending killing spree. Maybe I would find something on the internet. We all know how accurate the internet can be. I wouldn't find anything misleading on there at all. I didn't believe the trained professionals caring for me, but I believed the internet would have the answers.

In all reality I was afraid of what I could possibly see or read. There were certain words that would trigger the worst anxiety in me. Murder, killing, suicide, knives, guns, death, psychotic or psychosis, schizophrenia, infanticide and the list could go on forever. Anything that had to do with death or harm scared the hell out of me. I was still hiding the knives in my kitchen. In my heart I knew that I wasn't capable of doing any of those horrible things that were going through my mind, but the "what-ifs" would come into play and drive me crazy.

As I mentioned earlier, the one subject that I was petrified to hear or read about was the story of Andrea Yates. In the beginning of my illness I had gone to a website about her and only focused on postpartum psychosis and the deaths of her children. It was absolutely horrific. I needed to know more. I had to face my fears, read about her life and the series of events that occurred before she had killed her own children. So I did some research, even though it would cause me much distress. I wanted to see if there were any similarities between her and I.

Andrea (Kennedy) Yates was born on July 2, 1964, in Houston, Texas and was raised Catholic. She graduated from Milby High School in Houston in 1982. She was the class valedictorian, captain of the swim team and an officer in the National Honor Society. She completed a two-year pre-nursing program at the University of Houston and then graduated in 1986 from the University of Texas, School of Nursing. She worked as a registered nurse at the University of Texas M.D. Anderson Cancer Center from 1986 until 1994.

Andrea

Andrea and Rusty Yates, both 25, met at their apartment complex in Houston. Andrea, who was usually reserved, initiated the conversation. Andrea had never dated anyone until she turned 23, and prior to meeting Rusty, she was healing from a broken relationship. They eventually moved in together and spent much of their time involved in religious study and prayer.

They were married on April 17, 1993. At their wedding, they shared their plans to have as many children as nature provided. In their eight years of marriage, the Yateses had five children; four boys and one girl. Andrea stopped jogging and swimming when she became pregnant with her second child. Friends say that she became reclusive. The decision to home-school the children seemed to feed her isolation.

This is a brief timeline of what happened:
- February 17, 1993, Noah Jack Yates was born.
- December 15, 1995, John Samuel Yates was born.
- November, 1996, Andrea had a miscarriage.
- September 13, 1997, Paul Abraham Yates was born.
- February 15, 1999, Luke David Yates was born.
- June 17, 1999, Andrea Yates overdosed on trazodone.
- June 17-24, 1999, Andrea's first hospitalization. Diagnosis: "major depressive disorder, single episode, severe."
- July 20, 1999, Andrea attempts to kill herself with a knife.
- July 21- August 8, 1999, Andrea's second hospitalization. Diagnosis: "major depressive disorder, severe, recurrent, with psychotic features. Rule out schizophrenia, catatonic type."

1. About Inc., A part of The New York Times Company. 2006. http://crime.about.com/od/current/p/andreayates.htm

Wendy Isnardi

- August 9-20, 1999, Andrea continues hospital care as a day patient.
- October, 1999, Andrea's Haldol/Decanoate injections were discontinued. *Haldol is used to reduce the symptoms of mental disorders such as schizophrenia. It is also prescribed to control tics (uncontrolled muscle contractions of face, arms, or shoulders) and the unintended utterances that mark Gilles de la Tourettes syndrome.*[1]
- January, 2000, Andrea's last monthly visit with psychiatrist Eileen Starbranch.
- November 30, 2000, Mary Deborah Yates was born.
- March 12, 2001, Andrea's father dies.
- March 31 - April 12, 2001, Andrea's third hospitalization. Diagnosis: "postpartum depression. Major depression, recurrent. Rule out psychotic features."
- April 2, 2001, Andrea's psychiatrist Mohammad Saeed, MD, requested her court-ordered commitment to Austin State Hospital. Diagnosis: "Major depression, with psychotic features."
- April 13, 2001, Andrea is admitted as a day patient at a treatment center.
- May 4 - 14, 2001, Andrea's fourth hospitalization. Diagnosis: "postpartum depression" and "major depression recurrent severe (postpartum)." Haldol prescribed for second time in Andrea's medical history.
- June 4, 2001, Psychiatrist Mohammad Saeed ordered Andrea to discontinue Haldol and did not prescribe another antipsychotic medication only weeks before being allowed to receive care as a day patient at hospital.

2. About Inc., A part of The New York Times Company. 2006. http://crime.about.com/od/current/p/andreayates.htm

150

Andrea

- June 18, 2001, Andrea's last appointment with psychiatrist Mohammad Saeed.
- June 20, 2001, Andrea drowns her five children in the bathtub of her home.

After reading and doing research on Andrea Yates, I couldn't believe how she slipped through the system. As I got better, I was able to find out more in-depth information on her case. She was an extremely ill woman who needed to stay in the care of competent doctors. This tragedy was so easily avoidable.

Andrea's condition didn't just happen overnight. She was very ill for a long time. It is documented that she experienced her first bout with depression when she was 24 after a failed relationship. In addition, they also found that she has a brother who is bipolar. Her other brother and possibly her father suffered from depression as well, so there was a family history of mental illness.

Andrea and Rusty planned on having as many children as God sent their way. In 1994 after the birth of her first child, Noah, Andrea quit her job to become a stay-at-home mom. From that point on, she was having violent visions and hearing Satan, and she didn't tell anyone. She didn't get help until June of 1999, when she attempted suicide by taking 40 trazodone tablets.

Andrea was also extremely influenced by a preacher, who was very critical of mothers who believe in Jesus and the New Testament. They had purchased the trailer they lived in from this preacher. He denounced Catholicism (Andrea was raised Catholic), warning of their banishment to Hell. She became obsessed with reading the Bible. At the time she killed her children, she believed that Satan was inside of her and had irrevocably damaged her children.

Andrea was prescribed various antipsychotic and depression medications, some of which she would take half doses of or skip altogether. She was hearing voices and seeing visions. She was hospitalized four times and attempted suicide on several occasions. She had five children and one miscarriage in six years. That is unbelievable. On top of everything, she home-schooled her children and at one time lived in a small trailer with her family.

Another issue was that Andrea's father had died four months after the birth of her fifth child. She had also been taken off her much needed antipsychotic medication and was released from the hospital days before she committed these horrible crimes.

It's no wonder she went off the deep end. One could go crazy thinking of other possible outcomes if she hadn't been released from the hospital, been left home alone, or kept on the medication she needed.

After educating myself a bit, I felt a little relieved but still afraid that there was a small possibility that it could happen to me. There were no similarities between Andrea and I; I was confident about that. My fear was my indecisiveness, which was a result of the OCD; I doubted everything. Life has no guarantees, and I was not much of an optimist at that time. The glass was always half empty. So I would ask myself, *What is the difference between Andrea and I?* I wouldn't find out or really understand until I got better.

Circle of Caring

I had two choices: crawl into a ball and let this nightmare get the best of me until I was dead, or get ahold of myself and fight for my life. Obviously, I chose the second option. I couldn't let this happen to me; I was stronger than that. It was time to take the bull by the horns and get my life back. My pessimism was beginning to turn into optimism. I had to get better; there was no other option. I had too much to live for.

In my sessions with Irene, we worked on my mothering skills. I remember Irene saying, "It's time to face your fears." I had to bathe, feed, change and clothe Madison. Every week, I had a new assignment. The thoughts were still there, but I had to overcome them. "A thought is just thought," Irene would say. One of the methods we used was "thought stopping." I would wear a rubber band around my wrist, and anytime I would have a bad thought, I would snap the rubber band to divert the thought process. It worked from time to time. I would get the craziest looks from my family because out of nowhere, I would start snapping this rubber band. It hurt really badly, and I had some welts on my arm, but I had to suck it up.

My first assignment was to dress Madison on my own. I had a very hard time putting clothing over her head, so I was just putting everything on her from the bottom up. I was afraid that I would accidentally hurt her little head while I was dressing her. Her head and neck were tiny and delicate and seemed so fragile. It seemed as if her neck would just break. I had to realize that she wasn't made of twigs; she was a baby. Mothers have been dressing babies since the beginning of time, so what the hell was my problem? I had to face my fears, and guess what happened? Absolutely nothing! It wasn't easy in the beginning, and it took some time before the anxiety went away, but after a while, I was fine. The dressing process was quick and easy, and her head didn't fall off.

Feeding, and changing Madison's diaper was a breeze. I never used the changing table for fear that she would fall off and crack her head open or break something, and I hated using the straps because I thought she would strangle herself. I would change her on the floor, but that wasn't part of the assignment. I had to change her on the table and realize that she wasn't going to fall off or strangle herself.

My coping skills were improving, but I was far from cured. I was an emotional cripple. I think I had convinced myself that I would be a miserable person and an emotionless mother for the rest of my life. I definitely didn't think I would ever have or want any more children.

By the beginning of October, the Circle of Caring group had started. The Circle of Caring group was an offering of the Postpartum

Resource Center. It was a support group for mothers suffering with postpartum depression. I was so excited on the first day the group met. I was just really upset that the group would only meet once a week for an hour and a half. I felt like I was going out on the town. In all reality, I was meeting with a group of women who were miserable, just like me. For the first time in two months, I was looking forward to something and had several moments of happiness that day.

Sonia suggested that I bring Madison with me to the group. There were going to be seven or eight other mothers attending the meeting, which put me somewhat at ease. I got dressed and actually put on makeup; I hadn't done that in a long time. I picked out a really cute outfit for Madison and even dressed her myself. The meeting started at 7:30 p.m., and I got there at 7:00 p.m.

The group was held in a church. Before I went in, I sat in the parking lot for a few minutes. I was a little nervous, not knowing what to expect. I walked into a small room and was greeted by Sonia and a woman named Emily Sampino. Emily co-founded the Resource Center with Sonia in 1998. Sonia briefly talked about Emily to me on the phone. Emily had suffered from PPD after the birth of her first child. Amazingly, Emily and Sonia's paths crossed resulting in the Postpartum Resource Center. Thank God!

The Circle of Caring was set in a circle. Sonia and Emily sat directly across from each other and everyone else was connecting with them. I think that each mother was fighting back her tears, myself included. Most of the moms had their babies in carriers on the floor in front of them. I stared at every mother, wondering what was going on in her head. Of course, I was suffering the most and was the only one who wasn't going to recover. When everyone arrived, we all introduced ourselves. Most of the moms were extremely emotional and became choked up when they spoke of their ordeal.

Then Sonia and Emily gave us a brief description about themselves. They handed out folders with several different forms in them for us to fill out. I looked around the room and noticed that I was the only mom with makeup on. I thought that putting on makeup would mask the pain I was feeling. Who was I kidding?

We got into detail about our situations, each varying in severity. Some of the moms didn't seem too bad, meaning they were still functioning. Some had overwhelming feelings of love for their babies, and a couple of moms were anxious messes. One of the mothers was so down and depressed that I was shocked she even made it to the meeting. She was extremely withdrawn and didn't speak at all, spending most of the session crying. Some were really young and some were in their 40s. Some worked, and some were stay-at-home moms. We all came from different financial backgrounds. Some mothers had a ton of support and some had none at all. Some of us were first-time moms and some had several children. Unbelievably, some of these moms had gone through this once or twice before. The universal feeling was just pure sadness and despair. The only thing that isolated me from the group was my obsessive-compulsive disorder. Though most of the moms were suffering from extreme anxiety, I was the only one who was lucky enough to be suffering from that gift.

As each of us went into detail about ourselves, I could see the true concern on the looks of Emily and Sonia's faces. After we finished our stories, Sonia and Emily went into their own personal stories in great detail. Sonia did not suffer from postpartum depression, but her sister Becky suffered from postpartum psychosis. After a horrible experience and Sonia's undying dedication to her sister, she went on to create the Postpartum Resource Center with Emily. Emily, who was a stockbroker, had gone through PPD very badly after the birth of her first child. It took her a very long time to find the help she needed. In a strange twist of fate, Emily and Sonia met in a postpartum depression internet chat room.

The hour and a half went by quickly. I didn't want to go home. I felt safe there. I was surrounded by people who didn't think I was insane. They were all going through the same hell I was experiencing. I would have to wait another week for us to meet again. The Circle of Caring group was fundamental to my recovery. The medication helped, and so did the therapy, but being around women who were going through the same experience I was, felt incalculable.

The experience and lessons learned from the group would change my life forever. There were times that I doubted myself, thinking there was no such thing as PPD, and maybe I was going through something else, but seeing these women made me realize that I wasn't alone.

The most memorable meeting was "family night." We had the opportunity to bring our husbands or caretakers to meet with other mothers who had recovered from postpartum depression and their families/caretakers. I didn't think that my husband was going to attend that event, but to my surprise, he did. My mother attended as well.

We were split up into two groups. One group was the PPD moms with the recovered PPD moms. The second group was the PPD families with the recovered PPD families. The two groups shared their stories, and after 45 minutes, the groups were split up again—the PPD moms went with the recovered PPD families and the PPD families with the recovered PPD moms. It was perfect because it enabled us to see all aspects of the illness and how it affects everyone. It was also very interesting getting the husbands' perspectives and perception.

I know that Joey got a lot of very useful information on the illness that he never knew before. I think that seeing the other mothers that had the same symptoms as I did and then hearing how they recovered validated the way I was feeling. Hearing the husbands' sides of the story and how they coped was even better. It gave Joey a sense of understanding; he wasn't the only man dealing with this either. Sooner than I expected, the group was coming to an end. It was the shortest eight weeks of my life. I thought that if all of the mothers complained enough that Sonia and Emily would extend the group. P.S.: they didn't. The group was only intended to be eight weeks long, and this was a non-profit organization, so the funding was not there to extend the program.

How Long Is This Going To Last?

Minute by minute was how I had to take each day. I knew that I was better than I was in August, but I still was not myself. Not yet. I was so doped up on medication that I couldn't feel anything. I was starting to fear that being on the meds was numbing me, impairing my ability to feel love or emotion. But I wouldn't dare come off of them. There was no way I was going to risk going back to where I started. I just remained a disconnected, emotionless freak. From time to time, I would get small "peeks" of my old self. They would last only a few minutes, but they reminded me of who I used to be. The little "peeks" also gave me hope to carry on.

The weather was changing, which meant the holidays were not too far behind, and I was dreading that. The holidays were a time of happiness, fun, friends and family, and I wanted nothing to do with that. I also had to prepare for Madison's christening. I had planned to be better by then, but I had a strange feeling that I wasn't going to be.

Joey and I had chosen my brother Michael and my Aunt Andrea to be the godparents. Andrea is my mother's younger sister and is my godmother too. We had asked the both of them to be godparents to Madison right before she was born. They doted on Madison from the second they met her, which was minutes after she was born, so we knew we made the right decision.

Both Michael and Andrea saw how happy I was right after Madison's birth and the first few weeks that followed. I had wanted a baby in the worst way. When Madison arrived, I fell head over heels in love with her. Then my world fell apart, and it was very hard for me to tell them how I felt. The shame was unbearable. I was Wendy! . . . Michael's little sister and Andrea's niece. I was the one who always laughed and made jokes. I was never depressed or down.

I slowly erased myself from everyone's life. I couldn't look my family members in their eyes; it was too painful. My mother had the job of "bad news bearer." I knew that she probably over exaggerated a bit, but I didn't really care.

The first time I met up with Michael since the incident was a bit strange. He's a man; he knows nothing about hormones and stuff like that, and I still wasn't sure what my mother told him. He had a very sincere look on his face, which meant my mother told him I was going off the deep end. Michael is my big brother; he's never sincere with me.

"You look great! How are you feeling?" He asked.

Obviously he was lying because I looked like total crap. But it was nice to hear.

"Thanks. I am feeling much better," I lied.

He was very understanding and seemed to know what he was talking about. I tried to reassure him that I wasn't going to slit my wrists or anything.

My aunt was a different story. She's a woman and a mother. She has hormones. My aunt and her family live in Brooklyn, which is about an hour and a half west of me. I needed a change in scenery, so my mom, Madison and I would travel out there once a week. For the first meeting with her, I was a mess. To make matters worse, my little cousin, Nicole, who is like a sister to me, was there, as I cried like a baby in her mother's arms. She looked horrified and didn't know how to react to the whole depressing scene. The last time I saw her I was so happy and joking around with her. My aunt had never experienced PPD herself, but knew a few women who did. That seemed to be the universal response from most people I spoke with; "I didn't go through it, but I know someone who did." I wanted to meet that "someone" because I felt so alone.

I would sit in a room with everyone staring at me. When I would look up, all the people had huge fake smiles on their faces. It was actually quite funny. My cousin Nicole, who was only thirteen at the time, looked at me like I was crazy. Before all this crap happened, we were the life of the party. We would have so much fun together, and now I couldn't control my tears. Our conversations went from boys and clothes to antidepressants and psychiatrists. I felt very detached from everyone, and they spoke to me like I was a child. I was depressed, not mentally retarded; I didn't suffer any brain damage.

Andrea thought it would be a good idea if we all got together to go shopping for Madison's christening outfit. She came out to Long Island with my cousin, and Madison, my mom and I, were going to have a little sleepover. I loved spending time with my aunt and cousin, especially when we would have little slumber parties. This time, I wasn't feeling the normal excitement that I would experience when we would spend time together. This made me feel more depressed and frustrated.

We went shopping at a local boutique that carried the most beautiful children's clothing. I was so unhappy. This was supposed to be a joyous occasion, and I wanted to run away from home. I lived for this crap—picking out outfits, cute little shoes and bonnets, but I couldn't care less. I didn't know where I wanted to be, but I knew it wasn't there. Even before Madison was born, I had all these ideas in my head of the perfect christening outfit. But once again, I was missing out because I was so depressed. The PPD sucked all of the life out of me.

My aunt did a wonderful job picking everything out. She bought the dress, shoes, bonnet, socks, coat, blanket and anything else one could possibly need for a christening. I was a big phony with a big forced smile on my face, faking my happiness.

Afterwards, we all went to the mall and walked around for lack of anything better to do. I hated the mall and everyone in it. Right after the mall outing, we went back to my house, where I stared into the distance and cried on occasion. I felt so much guilt because I knew that everyone was there for me. They were all so concerned.

Life was going on around me, and I couldn't be there to enjoy it. I was being tormented by horrible thoughts and depression. It was a constant battle from the moment I woke up until I closed my eyes to go to sleep. There were times that I would try to force myself to feel better. I would force myself to love and feel love in return, but it was impossible. I would pray silently to myself several times a day that some miracle would occur and I would just be the old "Wendy" again.

How Long Is This Going To Last?

Halloween was here, and I picked out a really adorable peapod bunting costume for Madison. It was a "first" in the line of firsts. She was truly the most adorable baby I had ever laid my eyes on. I despised myself because I didn't feel that bond—the motherly connection that I once had. I knew what it felt like, and all that I wanted in the world was to get it back. I would've given my arms and legs for its return.

Madison's eyes were so big and beautiful that they consumed her face. Her complexion was rosy and her lips were perfect little rosebuds. I had gone trick-or-treating with my friend Debbie and her two children. I am still not sure why I even went trick-or-treating with Madison, being that she was only three months old at the time. It wasn't like she was eating candy or anything. I guess I just needed to be out of my house.

I was really trying to come out of my shell. I needed to socialize, even though it was against everything that I felt. We had lived in our house for well over a year, and I hadn't spoken to one of my neighbors. I didn't even know what they looked like. I went from being fat and pregnant to not wanting to talk to anyone, then to being a severely depressed mother who wanted to slice my throat open. I didn't have it in me to be a social butterfly. Joey, Mr. Antisocial, was stirring up conversations with the neighbors, and I didn't exist at all.

One day, my next-door neighbor, Donna, came over and brought a beautiful arrangement of flowers. I had never said a peep to her, and here she was with a gift for me. I felt so bad. Faking my happiness again, I had to put on a smile because she had no idea what was going on with me. She was really very sweet. Donna would become one of my closest friends in the years that followed. A year later she told me she thought I was a real bitch until she got to know me and realized what I was going through. I wasn't being bitchy and antisocial; I was just being depressed.

I needed to do things that would make my days go by quicker. I read a lot of books on depression, motherhood and OCD. I would read them over and over again. I still wasn't sure if I was going to return to work. I felt so shitty, and I didn't think it was such a good idea to go back to the office just yet.

I needed a hobby. I wasn't a very creative person, or so I thought. My friend Amy had come over one day, and we had gone out shopping. While we were out, she asked if I minded if we stopped at a scrapbooking store. Scrapbooking? Who does that, and why would they want to?

Well, I changed my opinion quickly. The store was tiny but it was packed with "stuff." Little stickers, pens and specialty paper that went into these beautiful scrapbooks. I was taken aback. The theme in the store was "memories and family." That was what I needed. A memory book to help me remember and chronicle Madison's life. I felt like I had missed out on so much of her life as it was, and this was the perfect way for me to get it back.

I spent $300 on scrapbooking paraphernalia in that one store; $300 is a ton of money to spend on scrapbooking. And that was just the beginning. We stopped at three other stores after that. I was hooked, and now I was on a mission. The scrapbooking became part of my therapy, and it truly helped. I lived the first three months of Madison's life all over again through pictures. As I created each page, I cried my eyes out wanting to be back in that place where all of the pictures were taken. I was still wondering why this happened to me and feeling so much anger and regret.

The scrapbooking opened the floodgates for me. I began painting and doing crafts. I would spend my days traveling to all the different craft stores just buying all kinds of stuff. I said earlier that

I wasn't creative and that is the God's honest truth. I had a hard time using whiteout, and now, not to sound conceited, I am pretty damn talented.

I was eating right, taking vitamins, exercising, socializing, going to church, getting sunlight and sleeping, but I wasn't getting much better. Every time I would ask Sonia, Irene, Ilene or Dr. Abey how long it was going to take for me to feel like myself none of them would give me a definitive answer. The universal response was "Everyone is different. No one's recovery time is the same."

That was not the answer I wanted to hear.

Two Steps Forward 200 Steps Back

If you have never experienced depression before, there is no way you could understand it. Depression is something that doesn't just go away. I remember the comments· "just go get a facial," or "go buy something." If it was that easy, I wouldn't be writing this right now. It's horrible and incapacitating. Before going through depression, I would joke about it. I've had friends and family members that had committed suicide, and I could not comprehend why and how they could do that to themselves. I understand now.

As time progressed, I was noticing little reprieves from my depression. The anxiety and OCD was still going strong. I was slowly reaching the maximum dosage of Zoloft. I had gone through three menstrual cycles hoping that the regulation of my hormones would help my condition. I became so in tune with my body. I felt my moods changing from second to second. I was beginning to believe that the meds were not working. That worried me because I really didn't want to start on a new medication. It would be like starting all over again, and what if a new medication didn't work on me either?

I had gone to my primary care physician because I had a bad sinus infection. While I was there, I explained my newly found PPD condition to her. I was still desperate for help, maybe there was something she could do to help me. She suggested that I go get a full blood workup done and have my thyroid checked. Sonia had mentioned to me that I should get my thyroid checked back in August, but I never went for the blood test, so this was a sign that maybe I should go and do it. Off to the lab I went.

After about a week the blood test results came in and it turned out that I had a thyroid problem. I had to make an appointment to see an endocrinologist who diagnosed me with postpartum thyroiditis. Who knew there was even such a thing? But I had it. Now the newest addition to my medication cocktail was Synthroid. The thyroid problem was definitely adding to my hormone fluctuation. Hopefully this new medication would help straighten me out.

By the beginning of November, I was really noticing a difference in my mood. This time it was for the better. Eureka! I was so excited. Was this nightmare coming to an end? I was becoming ambitious and started looking forward to things, and that was an emotion that I longed for.

Madison's christening was planned for the second week of November. It was nice to be able to participate in the preparation. It was something else to occupy my time. If this had been a month earlier, I don't think I would've been able to handle it.

Life was as strange and unpredictable as ever, but there was something new happening. My husband was not very close with his family. His father had died when he was only seventeen years old. Very soon after, he moved out on his own and didn't keep in contact with his mother or sisters. He felt very disconnected from his family. They had a very unconventional relationship. It wasn't the typical family setting. There weren't too many kisses and I love you's given out. They weren't that kind of family. Since his father passed, Joey was the only man in a house filled with women. It was his mother, three sisters and two nieces living under one roof. Way too many hormones for him.

When Joey and I started dating, he would speak with his mother on rare occasions. We were dating for six months already when I finally met her. Joey kept in touch with his two young nieces that lived with his mother, and that was only because I made him. I came from a very close-knit family, so the distance between them was not acceptable to me. We would disagree often, but I would make him visit her.

Once day we received a phone call from his sister Bernadette, saying that they were rushing his mother, Lucinda, to the hospital. She had been bleeding from her rectum and experiencing some pain for some time; she just assumed that it was hemorrhoids. Bernadette had called us from the emergency room to tell us that they were admitting Lucinda into the hospital for observation. They had found a blockage in her large intestine. My husband felt that she was fine and didn't think it was necessary for us to go to the hospital. Within one day, the doctors had decided to do surgery and found a very large tumor in her colon. She had very advanced colon cancer that had spread to her lymph nodes, and her chance of survival was slim.

Although Joey was not very close with his mother, this horrible unfortunate circumstance changed everything. We became a family. Going through PPD, I had no desire to talk to anyone. I felt that I alienated his family because I didn't think they would understand what I was going through. But now things had changed. Joey's family needed me, and I was preparing myself to be there for them. I would spend my days in the hospital watching television, reading and just hanging out with Lucinda. The medical staff allowed me to bring Madison into her room, and that made my mother-in-law very happy. Being with my mother-in-law and helping her was helping me as well. It definitely consumed a lot of time, and I enjoyed being with her. My mother finally got the opportunity to meet Joe's mother in the hospital. It was a strange way to begin a relationship, but they hit it off and had a lot in common. They both loved to knit and crochet, so my mother would come by the hospital a few times a week, and they would crochet together.

Around that time, we had celebrated Madison's christening, and unfortunately, Lucinda was in the hospital. The ceremony was beautiful, and Madison looked like an angel. I wasn't 100 percent Wendy, and that really aggravated me, but I had to take what I could get. Life was going on, and I was powerless to stop it. So I just went with the flow. That also became one of the beautiful memories that I would visit in my scrapbook.

Lucinda's health was deteriorating. The cancer had metastasized to her liver and pancreas. She spent Thanksgiving in the hospital and was going to start radiation treatment and chemotherapy in the beginning of December. I am still not sure if Lucinda or my sisters-in-law understood or realized the severity of the situation, but Joe and I knew exactly what was going on. She was dying.

We celebrated Thanksgiving with my parents that year. Lucinda was still in the hospital, so we visited her during the day. This was another first for Madison. My mood was the same. I wasn't as depressed, but I wasn't feeling anything. I am not sure which one is worse.

Through all this I was having peeks of Wendy. Peeks of how it should feel to be a mother. They were like cruel little tricks from the heavens. Just when I thought I was getting better, I would fall back into that horrible place.

What Doesn't Kill Us Makes Us Stronger

*L*ucinda was released from the hospital at the end of November. I helped my sisters-in-law with the responsibility of taking her back and forth to all of her appointments, which were plenty. Sadly, taking my mother-in-law to her appointments made me feel better. I guess it consumed my time and helped me concentrate on something other than the depression. By the second week of December, she was back in the hospital to have a colostomy bag put in.

One Saturday morning had started out like any "normal" Saturday for me. I had an appointment at 11:00 a.m. with Irene, a 12:30 p.m. appointment with Dr. Abey, and then I was going to the hospital to visit Lucinda with Madison. This morning, I also had my two nieces, Crystal and Elizabeth, so I would be taking them along for the ride.

Around 10:00 a.m., I received an alarming call

from Joey. He told me that he heard a call over the radio while he was at work. There was an unresponsive male at the address two houses away from my mother's house. He told me to go there right away.

It was my best friend's parents' house. I could tell by the urgency in Joey's voice that it was very serious. I got Madison bundled up and told my nieces to get in the car, then we rushed to the house. When we arrived at the residence, it was surrounded with emergency personnel. I parked my car in the middle of the street and left Madison with Crystal and Liz.

I left my house in such a rush that I didn't even change out of my pajamas and slippers. To make matters worse, there was about two feet of snow on the ground. I marched my way up the front lawn, losing one of my slippers in the snow. When I got into the house, the paramedics were working on Stacy's father, Ron, in the living room. I ran to Stacy's mother, Phyllis, and hugged her. She seemed to be in shock and asked me if I had spoken to Stacy, and I hadn't. I had been calling her home and cell phone every minute since receiving the call from Joey. Stacy and her fiancée, John, were on their way upstate for a family party that Ron and Phyllis were planning on going to as well. Stacy didn't have her cell phone on, so she couldn't be reached.

I couldn't believe my eyes, and I refused to accept what was going on in front of me. There wasn't any more they could do for Ron in their house, so he was being taken to the hospital by ambulance. Mind-bogglingly, no one else in the neighborhood knew what was happening. I was frantic and crying, so I just ran from door to door in my pajamas, telling the neighbors. The community was extremely close-knit, and everyone had known both Ron and Phyllis for at least thirty years, so I felt it was in everyone's best interest.

What Doesn't Kill Us Makes Us Stronger

I wanted to go to the hospital to meet the ambulance, but again, I was in my pajamas with one slipper on. I ran into my mother's house and got myself a pair of shoes, then ran back to my car, which was still in the middle of the street with my two nieces and Madison. Off we went to the hospital.

By the time I reached the hospital, Ron had passed. He died of a massive heart attack. I was devastated. That was a huge smack into reality and an eye opener for me. I had never lost anyone so close to me before, and to make matters worse, Stacy had no idea what was going on.

I stayed at the hospital in the waiting area with Madison, Crystal and Liz. Ironically, Lucinda was in the same hospital. I was trying to reach my mother and Stacy, but to no avail. I couldn't even go up to see my mother-in-law because I had the girls with me. At this hospital stay, they would not allow me to bring any children up into Lucinda's room.

When my mother came to visit Lucinda, she had no idea what happened to Ron. It was just coincidence that we were there at the same time. My mother was her usual happy self, ready to crochet with Lucinda, and I stopped her dead in her tracks. The news was shocking, and my mother and I had a breakdown in the lobby. Stacy and her family lived two houses away from my mother for years. Stacy practically lived at my mother's house when we were growing up. Stacy was like another daughter to my mom. Our parents shared many memories together over the years.

I needed to speak to an adult. For two hours, I was surrounded by two teenagers and a three-month-old. I had to be strong and keep my composure for them. They had no idea what the hell was going on; they didn't even know who Ron was.

I finally reached Stacy, and she already heard the horrible news.

My heart was completely broken. I was at a loss for words. This was my best friend, and I didn't know what to say to her. I just held the phone to my ear and listened to her cry. I wiped my tears and went back into the hospital so I could see my mother-in-law.

The days that followed were very difficult to say the least. Stacy and I had been through some very tough times together, but this was the worst. The funeral was just awful, watching Stacy and her family go through so much grief. My heart felt like it was ripped out of my chest and stepped on. I wanted to take all of her pain away, but I couldn't.

Just days after that, both of my grandparents went to the hospital with chest pains. First my grandfather, then about a day later my grandmother followed. Both had surgery in different hospitals; my grandfather had an angioplasty, and my grandmother got a pacemaker.

My best friend's father died, my mother-in-law was in the hospital with terminal cancer, both of my grandparents were in the hospital having heart surgery and I was in the throes of postpartum depression. What could possibly happen next?

It's a New Year

*C*hristmas came and went. My mother-in-law was out of the hospital and spent the holiday with us. There was so much going on that consumed my every day. My grandparents were out of the hospital and recovering. I tried to spend as much time with Stacy as I could because she was really having a hard time with everything, not to mention her wedding was five months away.

I rang in the New Year with friends and family. At the stroke of midnight, I hugged my husband and kissed my sleeping baby on her head. I was crying, but this time they were tears of joy. Everything had changed; I was a different person now. The recovery was a long and hard journey. I knew that I wasn't completely out of the woods just yet, but I was really close to it.

I had so much to be thankful for. I was really beginning to feel better. The "peeks" were longer.

Instead of lasting minutes, they were lasting hours, sometimes days. I was enjoying every second I had with Madison. I wasn't afraid to be alone anymore. The anxiety was still there, but I could handle it. The OCD thoughts were there, but I was learning how to dismiss them. The worst was certainly behind me. Looking back, four short months before, I was on the verge of something horrible. It could have been a suicide attempt or a stay in a mental hospital. I went through Hell for the first three months when the PPD symptoms were severe, but I made it through, and I held on. I was a lot stronger than I gave myself credit for. Being independent did so much for my confidence and self esteem.

When I awoke every morning, the first thought wasn't "Oh my God, I have postpartum depression, and I have to take my medication." Now my thoughts were more along the lines of "Oh my God, what am I going to do today? Will I go out with Madison or will we stay home?" Some days, I would even forget to take my medication. So right there, I knew that I was getting better. I even went as far as getting a tattoo on my lower back in celebration of Madison, and I am not a tattoo person. It will forever be a reminder of the hell I went through and the journey I took to get better.

I started feeling more like myself. When Joe would go to work I would take Madison shopping or we would just stay home and watch television or play. Our dog Petey was a big source of entertainment for her. He was a tiny ball of hair that loved to play and roll around. Just watching him frolic about made Madison crack up laughing. Her laugh was contagious.

I kept in touch with Sonia. We spoke often. I didn't forget my promise to her. Since I was feeling better, I was ready to fulfill my promise. I started to volunteer at the Resource Center by the end of January. I was doing simple tasks like answering the phones and entering data into the system. I even brought my mother along, and she became a volunteer too.

But I wanted to do more. Listening to the messages left by women was totally heartbreaking. It brought me back to that desperate time in my life, which wasn't too long ago. I was ready to take the next step and do phone support for the center. I was so inspired by Ilene, who was my phone support. She had no idea how much she helped me through my darkest days. Now, it was my turn to do the same for someone else, so I went for the necessary training needed to do it.

After my maternity leave was up, I had to make the decision whether or not I was going to go back to work. I was fortunate enough to have a choice and decided not to go back. I wanted to spend every second I could with Madison. I was different from other mothers. Mothers who have never gone through postpartum depression have no idea what it is like. They have no idea what it feels like to have their hearts ripped out of their chests with the inability to love or feel. They have no idea what it's like being unable to control emotions. They don't understand what it is when the joy of motherhood is taken away when new moms don't want to be alone with their beautiful new babies. It was hell, pure hell. A mother who has gone through PPD will love her baby more than a mother who hasn't gone through it. We know what it's like to have that love taken away. Once that love comes back, you never want to lose it again and would never take it for granted.

In February, I was taken off the Seroquel. I didn't need it anymore, thank goodness. The Seroquel was added when the anxiety was unbearable. It kicked in a lot quicker than the Zoloft did. Once I hit a therapeutic dose of Zoloft, I no longer needed to be on the Seroquel. I was seeing Irene and Dr. Abey once a month by choice. On a scale of one to ten, I was about a seven and a half. For someone who didn't think she was ever going to recover, that was pretty damn impressive.

Some would say I should have my head examined, but Joey and I decided to have an extension added to our house. It was a small three-bedroom ranch, but we added a second floor and then some. That meant that we had to completely move out of our house for at least two months and go live with my mom. It seemed like a really good idea at the time.

At the beginning of March, we packed up our stuff and moved out. After the first day of construction, my house was completely gutted, and there was no turning back.

Now, Joey, Madison, Petey-dog and I moved into my old bedroom in my mother's house. For the first few weeks, it was fun, but very soon after, it became a nuisance. We had no privacy at all. I wanted my house back, and it was nowhere near done.

The sperm donor's construction company was doing the extension, and I harassed him every day. Some days, I would pack a lunch and camp out on my front lawn with Madison, watching the men work, hoping that by some miracle they would get it done sooner. Some days, Lucinda would sit on the front lawn with me and watch the construction, but she was getting worse. Day by day, we watched her deteriorate. In and out of the hospital she went. Around April, she was released from the hospital, and hospice was called. It was only a matter of time before she passed.

We all tried to make her days happy. My mother and Lucinda would crochet blankets. I would give her manicures and pedicures. My niece Liz would do her hair in different kinds of styles. Sadly, she would talk about the future, but I knew in my heart that she wouldn't be around, and that killed me. All she wanted to do was spend time with her family. She got such a kick out of Madison; she called her the "Chunky Tuna" because she had the chubbiest, most pinchable cheeks, and my mother-in-law ate them up. Spending time with her grandchildren made her so happy. It was the simple things in life.

By May, we were still living in my mother's house and completely losing our minds. Our house was close to being done, but not livable just yet. Stacy and her fiancée were getting married on the 17th of that month, and I was the Maid of Honor. I was planning her bridal shower and bachelorette party—on top of everything else that was going on—and we decided to stay overnight in Atlantic City for the bachelorette party. This was the first time that I had ever been away from Madison for more than five hours, let alone overnight. The day before our trip, I was a nervous wreck. I couldn't stop crying, just thinking about being away from her for that long. Oddly enough, that was the emotion that I longed for while I was in the midst of depression. Now it was there, and it was so real and so strong.

The trip itself was fun. I think I needed to get away for a few days and be with my friends, but I couldn't wait to get home and hug my Madison. I thought about her constantly. I knew she was safe at home with her daddy, but I couldn't wait to see her.

Shortly after was Stacy's wedding, and it was extremely difficult. It was only five months since Stacy's father had passed away. The wedding was beautiful, and Stacy looked like a princess. Watching her walk down the aisle with her mother was very sad. There wasn't a dry eye in the room. To make matters worse, Stacy danced with her mother to "Wind Beneath My Wings." They were hugging and crying in the center of the dance floor. I think I had a mini-nervous breakdown. I actually ran out of the hall and cried my eyes out in the bathroom. I was a babbling fool. I got stuck in a groove and couldn't get out. At one point Stacy was consoling me, and that was odd because I was crying for her loss. For the longest time when I was suffering with the PPD, it was very hard for me to feel any emotion other then the horrible depression I experienced day in and day out. Now I was overwhelmed with emotions, but this time it was good. I was able to feel compassion, love and loss. It was like it was my wedding and my father had died.

On May 20 2003, we went to my mother-in-law's house for dinner. Joe, Madison, Bernadette, my other sister-in-law Cynthia, Crystal, Liz, and I were all there. Lucinda was falling in and out of consciousness, which had become the norm. The hospice nurse was there for a good portion of the day but left around 6:00 p.m.

Just as we sat down to eat dinner, we heard a strange gargling noise coming from the living room. Lucinda was throwing up what appeared to be thick coffee grounds. It just kept coming out of her. I will never forget the blank look on her face as she vomited. We called the hospice nurse back, and she made it over in about fifteen minutes. There wasn't anything that she could do, so we cleaned Lucinda up and changed her clothes and bedding. The nurse told us that it was only a matter of a week or so before she would pass.

Something just didn't feel right, so Joey and I decided to stay the night to keep an eye on my mother-in-law. It wasn't the best place for Madison to be, so I called my mother over to come get her. We all took turns sitting by her bed that night. Finally, around 12:30 a.m., Joey and I went to sleep in my niece's bedroom. About a half hour later, Cynthia was screaming for Joey. I knew in my heart that she was gone. Joey ran downstairs, and I stayed in the bedroom with Liz and Crystal. My instincts were right; Lucinda had passed.

The horrible screams I heard coming up from downstairs gave me the chills. I tried to keep it together for my two nieces, but it was really difficult. They were hysterical and wanted to see their grandmother. I remember taking them downstairs and seeing Lucinda's lifeless body lying there in the bed. I had such an uncomfortable feeling. I had been to funerals before and seen dead bodies, but this was different. She died in the house only minutes before I had come downstairs. Her eyes were still open. I wanted her to come back! I wanted her to be alert and talking, but I would never hear her voice again. Joey called the coroner to come and remove her body. When the coroner pulled up, we were all sitting outside because no one wanted to be inside the house with Lucinda's body.

That was it. It was all over. Lucinda was gone, just like that. She was diagnosed with the cancer in November, and six months later, she died. My heart was broken once again, not only for me, but for Joey and the rest of his family. My husband was orphaned at 27.

The funeral was a blur. I had to be the pillar of strength for everyone. I am not even sure how I made it through myself, but I did it. If this had occurred eight months prior, I don't know what I would've done. I was so afraid all the stress and heartache that I had been through in the past few months was really going to take a toll on me, possibly sending me back to that horrible dark place I never wanted to see again. But it didn't, and I was okay. I guess the combination of medication and therapy was doing the trick.

By the very end of May, we were back in our house. It was great. We kept busy by furnishing and decorating the house. We were also preparing for Madison's first birthday. We were planning a huge party in our yard. This was going to be a big celebration, and I wanted everything to be perfect, not to mention my own little personal victory. I was celebrating Madison's birthday and my recovery. There were times in the beginning when I didn't think I was going to be around for her first birthday. The thoughts of suicide were strong because I was so sad. But I did make it, and I was so grateful for that.

Madison's party was a hit. We had over 100 guests at our house. It was the huge celebration we wished for, and I enjoyed every second.

The light at the end of my tunnel was bright and I was nearing the end of the horrible journey. Life was very close to perfect and I had all of my family and friends to enjoy it with me . . .

The Dream Team

I said earlier, if and when I recovered from the PPD, I promised Sonia that I would do whatever it took to help other families suffering from the disorder. After I was trained for phone support for the Resource Center, I was ready to go. I wanted to make a difference, and doing the phone support was an effective way for me to help.

When I was sick with the PPD, it was so hard for me to talk to my friends and family because they could not relate to my situation. It was such a relief to speak to the other mothers in the program because they had been to that dark place. Once I got in touch with Ilene, my main phone support, I connected with her immediately. Speaking to Ilene was one of the only things I looked forward to when I was at my worst. I wanted to be that person for someone else.

I was a little nervous and unsure when

I received my first call, but as I listened to the desperation in the woman's voice, I knew I had made the right decision. I was on the phone with her for over an hour. I can honestly say that I felt her pain and wouldn't get off the phone with her until I knew she was okay.

I had some very busy days on the phone, speaking with mothers and sometimes their family members. It became my mission in life. Some days, I would speak with four and five mothers. Some would call several times in the day. I also had a lot of repeat callers, and it made me feel good that they were comfortable talking with me and valued my support. Many of the mothers were suffering in varying intensities; some were a bit more severe than others. They were all in my thoughts every day. Our conversations were all different in content. Some times, we would talk about everything but PPD. But most of the conversations revolved around medication, recovery, getting better, how I got better, fearing they would never love their babies again and Andrea Yates/psychosis.

Medication

I really tried my hardest to steer away from the medication topic, but unfortunately it always came up. It was such a hard subject to discuss. With my experience, every woman was different. Some took several medications, some took none, and some used vitamins and exercise. I couldn't give an opinion or advice that way. I wasn't a doctor, nor was I pretending to be. Zoloft was the medication for me, but that didn't mean that it would work for someone else. There were many mothers who had taken Zoloft and found it ineffective. I was lucky that I found a medication that worked. Some mothers had taken a shopping list of medications to no benefit. Nothing seemed to work, and they were completely frustrated.

Several mothers were breastfeeding and refused to take medication while they were nursing for fear that the medication would somehow affect the baby. I give them a lot of credit. Yet there were some mothers on medication who breastfed with no bad affects on the baby at all. I found that those mothers recovered quicker than the moms not taking meds at all. All of the mothers who were breastfeeding had the same rationale. They all felt that breastfeeding was the only thing they had left bonding them to their babies. That was one issue that I knew little about, because I did not breastfeed. I chose not to breastfeed way before I gave birth. It was more of a personal preference for me. I remember a very close friend of mine who was trying to breastfeed, and she had such a hard time. She called me crying because she was in such pain, and she told me that her nipples were so sore that they bled. That was all I needed to hear. I got a visual in my head, and that was it. There will be no breastfeeding for me . . .

How long is this going to last?

That was an extremely common subject that I didn't have a decisive answer for. My response was the exact same one that I got when I was going through PPD: "Everyone is different. No one's recovery time is the same." When I gave that answer, I would hear the disappointment in their voices. I knew from my own encounter how discouraging it was to hear, but it was true.

I have spoken to women who start taking their medication on a Monday, and feel better by Friday (that's amazing; not common, but possible). Some women take months, and some take weeks. The one thing I knew for sure was that they all got better—medicated or not. Another message I try to convey is how crucial it is to seek help, see a medical professional and definitely try to find a support group as soon as possible. Don't wait and don't be ashamed or afraid to speak out.

How I Got Better!

Time, patience and education. I lived by the "Steps to Wellness." Time was my worst enemy and my best friend. It's all that I had, so I had to use it to my advantage. I made sure that I went to all my appointments with my therapist and psychiatrist. Joining the support group helped tremendously. I ate right, exercised and stayed away from alcohol. I took my medication at the same time every day. Most importantly, I got as much sleep as I possibly could.

I read every book published on postpartum depression, depression and its influence on anxiety disorders, and obsessive-compulsive disorder. It really took up a lot of time in my day. I also found my creative side. When one is bored and losing one's mind, she will do anything to help time go by. I changed my whole outlook on things. Instead of waking up feeling awful with no end in sight, I turned it around so each day was bringing me closer to my recovery.

I became very attuned to my body. I realized that my mood changed around the time I ovulated, when I was premenstrual and right after I menstruated. I prepared myself for the roller coaster of emotions and the worsening of my OCD. I was fully aware that during these hormone fluctuations I wasn't going to feel 100 percent like myself and I should not get thrown off by the changes. All of this was temporary and would go away. As time went on, I got used to the hormonal changes. I also tried not to get myself too stressed out. The more I stressed, the stronger the anxiety and OCD thoughts would come.

Sleeping, eating well, exercising, relaxing and educating myself was the key to my recovery.

Will I Ever Love My Baby Again?

What kind of mother asks a question like that? The answer: a mother going through postpartum depression. That is, in my opinion, the worst problem with the illness. Motherhood is a gift and a blessing. To be hit with a horrible and debilitating illness right after childbirth that incapacitates a mother's ability to care for her own child is terrifying, and the only way to understand that dreadful feeling is if you experience it firsthand. I knew exactly what these mothers were talking about because I had been there. The guilt these unfortunate women feel is overwhelming. That is when the tears and the pain come into play. Most mothers are fine during our conversation. Then the crying starts when they discuss the inability to feel love for their baby. They feel dreadful.

The best answer I could give was the answer given to me. I remember crying to Sonia, trying to make sense of the horrible thoughts. I could handle not feeling any love for my husband or the rest of my family, but *not* Madison. What kind of mother was I? Maybe I didn't deserve her. Maybe I shouldn't have been a mother. Maybe I was a monster. Sonia's response was: "You love Madison very much. Everything that you do everyday proves how much you love her. If you didn't care or love her you wouldn't be on the phone with me. You wouldn't be seeking help from any doctor or therapist. You would do nothing."

That was so true. If I didn't love Madison I wouldn't have gotten any help at all. I would just go on doing nothing. I would go out with friends or do everything except try to get better. I have stolen Sonia's line and use it when I speak to other moms. And guess what? It works because it's true.

Andrea Yates & Psychosis

Andrea and psychosis are mentioned in every conversation. I find the frequency of phone calls increases when the medias attention is on Andrea Yates or some other tragedy as a result of postpartum depression. I go back and remember conversations that I had with my therapist and doctors over the fear of becoming psychotic. That is the worst possible outcome of the illness. That's just the worst possible outcome, period.

Most mothers are confident that nothing will happen to them or their baby as long as they are in control of themselves. It's the "psychosis" factor that comes into play. "How does that happen and how can anyone be sure that's not going to happen to them?" I think I asked that question a million times myself.

Then they would ask about Andrea Yates. I try to explain how truly ill she was and that she should not have been released from the hospital or taken off the medication she needed. That tragedy was extremely avoidable and should've never happened.

The only way I could satisfy my own curiosity was to educate myself and learn the facts. Psychosis is a very scary thing. It's no wonder a mother would worry about the possibility of that occurring. Most of the women that I spoke to were at no risk whatsoever of becoming psychotic. I just tried to put their minds at ease that they weren't at any risk, but to be on the safe side, consult their doctor if they were concerned.

Signs of Postpartum Psychosis

Although the onset of symptoms can occur at any time within the first three months after giving birth, women who have postpartum psychosis usually develop symptoms within the first two to three weeks after delivery. Postpartum psychosis symptoms usually appear quite suddenly; in 80 percent of cases, the psychosis occurs three to fourteen days after a symptom-free period.

Signs of postpartum psychosis include:

Hallucinations

Delusions

Illogical thoughts

Insomnia

Refusing to eat

Extreme feelings of anxiety and agitation

Periods of delirium or mania

Suicidal or homicidal thoughts

Who is at Risk?

Women with a personal history of psychosis, bipolar disorder or schizophrenia have an increased risk of developing postpartum psychosis. Likewise, women who have a family history of psychosis, bipolar disorder or schizophrenia have a greater chance of developing the disorder.

Causes of Postpartum Psychosis

Experts aren't exactly sure why postpartum psychosis happens. However, they do offer a variety of explanations for the disorder, with a woman's changing hormones being at the top of their list. Other possible reasons or contributing factors include a lack of social and emotional support; a low sense of self-esteem due to a woman's postpartum appearance; feeling inadequate as a mother; feeling isolated and alone; having financial problems; and undergoing a major life change, such as moving or starting a new job.

My mother wanted to do her part, too. She became a volunteer and helped at the Resource Center doing data entry and helping with fundraisers. But we both wanted to do more. Sonia had asked us if we would be interested in speaking at the Circle of Caring meetings for family night. We automatically agreed. I had never been much of a public speaker and neither was my mom, but we let go of all of our insecurities for the cause. It was so strange being the support giver, but it was a great feeling making a difference.

That was the beginning for my mom and me. That was also when Sonia dubbed us the "dream team." We did everything together. We would speak at forums for various women's health agencies including: The Catholic Campaign For Human Development, Suffolk County Perinatal Coalition, Inc., Suffolk County Department of Health Services and The Mother's Center of the South Shore, just to name a few.

Then one day, Sonia asked me if I would be interested in doing an article for *Self* magazine. I was a little apprehensive at first. This was a bit different from the volunteering I was doing, but this was a chance for me to get my story out there, possibly making a difference in someone's life. So I said, "What the hell, why not?"

The article was about mothers suffering from postpartum depression and obsessive-compulsive disorder. It was a collaboration of stories told by other mothers and several healthcare professionals. The article was entitled "Will I Hurt the Baby?" was to be released in

The Dream Team

April 2006. I became concerned about the title for fear that people would read the article and think that I possibly wanted to harm my daughter. I wanted to make sure it was clear; at no time did I ever want to harm Madison. They were all just thoughts that terrified me. They terrified me, so I avoided being alone with my daughter for three months. But the woman who wrote the article did a wonderful job of making that point totally clear.

After several months of interviews and fact-finding, it was time for the article to be released. The only thing I disagreed with was allowing my picture to be posted in the article. I don't know why I didn't want it in the article. I think I was a little embarrassed that someone who knew me might recognize me. I feared that people might misinterpret the article and think I was a danger to society. Looking back, I really made a mistake.

Soon after the article's release, I started receiving phone calls from friends and family. I got such positive feedback from everyone, some of whom had no idea that I had even suffered from either illness. Most importantly, I helped other women who were going through the same thing I went through. To my amazement, I received another call from Sonia; this time, it was about appearing on *The Paula Zahn Show*. CNN had contacted the Resource Center about the article we did for *Self* magazine, and they were very interested and wanted to do a segment on the *Paula Zahn Show* about the article.

This was something entirely out of the ordinary for me. I wouldn't put a photograph of myself in a magazine, but now I was considering going on television. I discussed it with Joey, and we both decided it would be a good idea. Then reality set in, and I realized that I was going to be on television, not on some public access channel, but CNN. What the hell was I thinking? Was I insane? I wasn't insane; I was dedicated to a cause. I had to let go of all my insecurities now more than ever.

It's very difficult to announce to the whole world that you were severely depressed, taking antidepressant medication, afraid to be left alone and avoiding your own child. A good portion of the general public is not familiar with the illness, and there are a lot of people who frown upon taking antidepressant medication. I was going to have to prepare myself for all the comments.

But that was the reason I was doing this. I wanted my story to get out there. It shouldn't be a secret, and I definitely shouldn't be ashamed. I am not a murderer or a rapist. I am a mother who suffered from postpartum depression. Millions of women suffer in silence because they are afraid to tell anyone what they are feeling. I couldn't imagine not seeking help because of the fear of what everyone would think. Getting help was the best thing I did for Madison and myself.

Brooke Shields did such a wonderful service by putting her story out there. She made postpartum depression a household term; I guess one would say she normalized it. Brooke was very candid with her description of the horrors she went through and her journey to recovery. Society's image of a woman suffering from PPD was poor Andrea Yates. Now that image has changed.

The *Paula Zahn* crew showed up at my house bright and early for the taping. The camera crew came in with all of their equipment and started moving around furniture, taking control of the situation. I was upstairs getting Madison and myself ready. I had no idea what to wear or how to do my makeup and hair. They told me to look "normal" and not done up, so that's what I did; I made myself look as "normal" as possible. Madison is such a natural beauty so it didn't take much for me to get her ready.

My mother and Sonia were also speaking in the segment. They

both showed up around the same time. When I came downstairs, I had a house full of people. There were cameras and lights all over the place. They meant business. It was time to start the interview. It was so bizarre. I couldn't believe how nervous I was. I thought I was going to pass out. The correspondent doing the interview was Deborah Feyerick. She came in minutes before the interview started and walked around the house, trying to find the perfect spot to conduct the interview. The kitchen won; that was the spot. The interview started in there, and eight hours later, ended in my backyard. Eight hours of taping resulted in a five-minute interview. I have a newfound respect for cameramen.

This is a condensed version of the actual interview:

DEBORAH FEYERICK, CNN correspondent *[voice-over]*: Even before her daughter was born, Wendy Isnardi admits she was a worrier.

WENDY ISNARDI, *[suffers from PPD]*: I always worry about everything. I would be afraid that I left like a window open or a door unlocked or the oven on or an iron. I would go to work, leave my job, and come back home to make sure that I turned everything off, which I knew that I did.

FEYERICK: After giving birth to Madison four years ago, those worries turned very dark and very frightening. Wendy became obsessed. Something or someone, even Wendy herself, might hurt the baby.

ISNARDI: I was afraid that she would fall down the stairs. She would drown in the tub. Whether it was by me, by my husband, by somebody, I was just horribly—I was horrified.

FEYERICK: The violent thoughts kept playing in her mind, getting worse and worse.

ISNARDI: Every time I would try to, you know, stop the thoughts, they would just come on strong and the anxiety would get stronger and stronger.

FEYERICK: It got so bad, Wendy was afraid to be alone with her own child.

[On camera]: Did you think, oh, my God, could I be an Andrea Yates?

ISNARDI: Yes, of course. That was my worst fear. And I think that's why I kind of hid myself. I would just stay in my room and just be away from everything, because everything would be safe.

FEYERICK *[voice-over]*: Andrea Yates is the mother who drowned her five young children in the bath tub. Yates was diagnosed with postpartum psychosis. Wendy was not. Her problem was different, something more common than most people realize. It wasn't just postpartum depression, but postpartum OCD, obsessive-compulsive disorder triggered by the birth of her baby. Doctor Shari Lusskin is a psychiatrist who treats mental illness in new moms.

DR. SHARI LUSSKIN, NYU Medical Center: Up to 40 percent of mothers who have postpartum depression also have obsessive thoughts. And in general, in contrast to OCD in other situations, women who are postpartum have obsessions about the baby. So they worry in particular that they are going to do harm to the baby.

FEYERICK: That fear became so great, Wendy withdrew. Experts say that's a common reaction among new moms suffering from the disorder.

ISNARDI: I was scared to death. I didn't understand. I just cried.

FEYERICK: Wendy's husband, who is a police officer, and her mom, Pat, cared for the baby full-time almost three months.

[On camera]: Did you think that she could actually hurt the baby?

PAT GUTTILLA, Wendy's mother: Oh, no. No. I was more concerned that she would possibly hurt herself, not the baby.

SONIA MURDOCK, Postpartum Resource Center: The fears of OCD with moms are very, very real.

FEYERICK [voice-over]: Sonia Murdock runs the Postpartum Resource Center of New York, which is where she and Wendy first met.

[On camera]: Do these women fear that if they share their concerns, their thoughts, that their child might be taken from them?

MURDOCK: Absolutely. That is one of the greatest fears of moms going through postpartum OCD. They are afraid that they are going to be judged as bad people, bad mothers.

FEYERICK [voice-over]: Murdock and other experts say many women don't seek help because they are so ashamed of their own thoughts. But the overwhelming question is could these violent thoughts lead a woman to harm her own baby?

LUSSKIN: The short answer is, absolutely not. The hallmark of OCD is that the patient recognizes that the thoughts are illogical and, therefore, they won't act on them.

ISNARDI: I was so afraid, and I wanted to love her and hug her and kiss her, but I was afraid of, I don't know what.

FEYERICK: The first three months of her baby's life went by in a blur. That's when Wendy, a self-described perfectionist, reached out for help. Through her Lamaze coach, she got in touch with a therapist and a psychiatrist who put her on antianxiety medication.

ISNARDI: As soon as I started getting help and when I joined the group at the Resource Center, there were other women there, other mothers that were going through the same thing. And it made it more normal to me.

FEYERICK: Wendy now volunteers at the Postpartum Resource Center, talking to other women about her own experiences. As for

her daughter—

Isnardi: Got to move out of the way . . . when I come back, okay? *[pushing Madison on a swing]*

Feyerick: The fear of really hurting her is all but gone.

[On camera]: Do any of these thoughts come back?

Isnardi: Not really, no. I mean if they do, it's just a thought, and I just am able to, you know; just let it pass, just like anything else.

Feyerick: When you look at Madison now, are you afraid you're going to hurt her?

Isnardi: No, never. I love her so much. She is my life.

Feyerick *[voice-over]*: A life so precious Wendy and her husband are now talking about having a second child. Deborah Feyerick, CNN, New York.

The interview aired on April 19, 2006, about a week after the actual taping. If I thought I was nervous for the taping, I thought I was going to have a mental breakdown the day it aired. Everyone and their mother knew about the interview. What worried me was that I hadn't seen the interview yet. I had no idea what to expect.

It was very disturbing seeing myself on television like that. I thought I looked so strange. About one minute into the airing of the interview, my phone started to ring, and didn't stop until 11:30 p.m. Then phone calls continued the next morning. CNN kept airing the interview every hour. In addition, it was also being played on their website.

I got phone calls from people I hadn't spoken to in years. It was amazing how many people knew me at the time and had no idea what I was going through. Well, they knew now. Everyone did. I am amazed at how many people watch the news. I was going into stores and getting recognized. I was semi-famous.

There were some people, my husband's friends, who watched the interview and made fun of me. They would joke with their stupid comments and say, "I didn't realize that you were crazy Wendy," or "You don't want to kill your baby now, do you?" At first it bothered me, but after a while, I realized that none of it was true. I was never in any danger of harming Madison, let alone killing her, nor was I crazy. So they could joke as much as they wanted because I knew the truth.

The greatest gift of all was receiving calls from mothers suffering from PPD/OCD who watched the interview, telling me that I helped them. That meant the world to me. That's the reason I did it! Months later, CNN still broadcast the interview, and I got phone calls.

In May of 2006, I was asked to join The Suffolk County Perinatal Task Force, which I gladly accepted. The task force's mission is to explore and identify the needs of women in Suffolk County; advise the Suffolk County Office of Women's Services, The County Executive, and the Legislature of those findings; advocate for appropriate changes in policy and practices to meet those needs; coordinate and develop resources in both the public and private sectors; stimulate community awareness and interest in women's issues and in the resources available; ensure recognition of a response to the needs and accomplishments of Suffolk women; promote awareness concerning the most common medical complication related to having a baby—postpartum depression. As a result of our efforts, the County Executive Steve Levy declared the month of May and every year thereafter Perinatal Mood Disorders Awareness Month in Suffolk County.

Wendy Isnardi

The success of the postpartum program was celebrated at "The Spring Charity Dinner Theater," a fundraiser for the Postpartum Resource Center. It was such an honor to be involved and recognized for our accomplishments. Something wonderful and unexpected happened the night of that charity dinner. I was greeting everyone and checking their tickets before they entered the dining room. Then I heard a familiar voice, one that I hadn't heard in a long time. When I looked up, I didn't recognize her face, but when she told me her name, I knew. It was Ilene, my phone support, one of the women who very possibly saved my life in my time of need. I had never seen her before, but I could never forget her voice, even though I hadn't spoken to her in three years. I immediately introduced myself, and luckily she remembered me. My eyes welled up with tears, and I hugged her. Hearing her voice brought me back to that horrible place for a moment. I was so happy that I finally got to put the face with the voice.

Later on that evening I had to speak in front of the audience to tell my story once again. I couldn't help but mention Ilene and how she changed my life with her kind words, and I graciously thanked her. I think I may have embarrassed her, but I didn't care, she needed to know how appreciative I was of her. Besides, she was a big reason why I became a volunteer in the first place.

Volunteering has become a huge part of my life and I will do whatever it takes to help. I am currently The Resource Coordinator for the PRC and co-facilitate a support group for moms. What Sonia, Emily and the Resource Center gave me was and is invaluable.

So What Happened Next?

Well, after several conversations with Dr. Abey and Irene, Joey and I decided that we wanted to have another baby. I couldn't let what happened when I had Madison affect the rest of my life. This time around, I was aware of the possibilities and was prepared for the fight. I wasn't going to be blindsided. Joe and I wanted to have another child, God willing. Madison was three years old and kept asking for a new brother or sister. We had enough room in the house now for another child. I felt I was emotionally and mentally prepared for this huge step. Unfortunately, my original OB/GYN, Dr. Jean, was no longer practicing obstetrics, so I had to find another doctor. Dr. Jean referred me to a new doctor, one of his good friends and a trusted colleague.

I became pregnant right away. I sat down with my new OB/GYN and discussed my birth plan. Both Joey and I felt it was very important that I needed to stay on the medication. The doctor had his reservations and would discuss the medication options as the pregnancy progressed. For the time being, he would keep me on the meds, but at a lower dose.

From the start, I felt my mood changing by the second. I must admit that I was afraid. Waves of depression were flooding my day, but I was able to handle it. It was to be expected with all the changes in my hormones. I had the cutest little bump that seemed to form much quicker this time around. I had an extra baby book; I got it as a gift at Madison's baby shower, and I saved it just in case I had another baby. I already started filling it out, anticipating the new addition.

I was so excited going for my three-month checkup. Joe and I wanted Madison to be involved in the entire baby process, so we brought her along to the doctor's appointment. I couldn't wait for her to hear the baby's heartbeat and see the image on the sonogram. We sat patiently in the doctor's office while the doctor and the nurse prepared all the machines. Joey and Madison sat at my side as Madison held my hand tightly. The nurse poured the freezing cold sonogram gel all over my little bump and searched for the little baby in my belly, but something was wrong. We didn't see or hear anything. The doctor had a very troubled look on his face. He said, "There is no heartbeat. You have miscarried; I am so sorry."

I was in a complete state of shock and started sobbing uncontrollably. I tried to control myself because Madison was there and didn't understand what was going on. Mental note: don't take a three-year-old with you to a three-month checkup until you know everything is okay.

We sat in the doctor's office at his desk, and he tried to console me as best as he could. He explained that I had a partial molar pregnancy. He kept referring to the baby as a mole, which really confused me, as if I was going to give birth to some kind of hairy animal. A partial mole occurs when two sperm fertilize an egg. Instead of forming twins, something goes wrong, leading to a pregnancy of an abnormal fetus and an abnormal placenta. If the baby was to have lived, it would be born severely deformed. I had an incomplete miscarriage, so I had to go for a D and C (dilation and curettage). My appointment for the D and C wasn't scheduled for another week, so I had to walk around with a dead fetus. I was horrified.

Not only did I lose the baby, I would have to wait at least a year before I could try to become pregnant again. In addition, I would have to go for blood tests every month to check my HGC levels for gestational trophoblastic disease. Gestational trophoblastic disease is a growth of abnormal tissue inside the uterus during pregnancy. The tissue prevents the normal growth of a fetus and can continue to grow after a miscarriage. And in rare cases, gestational trophoblastic disease can advance into uterine cancer, which would be treated with chemotherapy. All I could process in my mind was the worst-case scenario.

I was totally devastated. I left the doctor's office and cried hysterically. I just couldn't control my emotions. My first phone call was to my mother. She knew how excited I was about going to the appointment with Maddy. As soon as she heard my voice, she knew something was wrong. Instead of the happy call she was expecting to get from me, she got me bawling inaudibly on the other end. I couldn't believe my own words. "I had a miscarriage." Now the both of us were crying.

I was really upset, but it wasn't a depression; it was a feeling of total loss. This time, I was upset because I lost our child, and I was fully aware that everything was going to be okay. I was mourning the baby that I would never get to meet. My mind was flooded with thoughts of what this baby would've looked like. Was it a girl or a boy? I woke up that day pregnant and now I wasn't. I was so extraordinarily miserable and sad.

We had a birthday party to go to that afternoon that I now had no desire to attend. The party was for a very close friend's daughter and we planned on going that very morning. I was excited to go so that I could share my happy baby "updates" with all of my friends who would be there. Instead, I had to have Joe say that we would not be attending because I lost the baby.

My mom had asked if we wanted her to watch Madison for the day so we could recover from the horrible reality that we had to process. We decided to spend the day together as a family. Joe figured we should go to the mall and walk around to keep our minds occupied. Madison still didn't really comprehend what had happened. Even though she knew I was very sad, she was resilient; all she wanted to do now was go to the toy store.

Mall + Mommy & Daddy = Toys.

All I could remember doing on our trip to the mall was staring out the window, sobbing uncontrollably. We didn't speak much, but Joe was sharing my misery and held my hand tightly the whole way.

Before we stopped at the mall, we made an unexpected stop at the jewelry store where Joe had purchased my engagement ring. I didn't even question why because my mind was a mushy mess. I figured we were stopping to get my ring reset and cleaned, which we would do from time to time. Like a robot, I pulled the ring off my finger and handed it to Joe. Madison was noticeably disappointed because she was certain that was not the toy store, so I picked her up and assured her that our next stop would be for toys!

So What Happened Next?

I roamed around the store aimlessly as Joe picked out jewelry that he thought was nice. I would look and nod with approval, not even expecting to get anything. He walked over to a showcase that had the most magnificent diamond bracelets. They were all so beautiful. I looked at them and blubbered all over the glass. The sales lady didn't know how to handle me. She was smart and stayed away.

I turned around and sat on a chair with Maddy on my lap. At that moment, I came to the realization that I may not be able to have any more children. I was grateful that I had this beautiful gift in Madison, and maybe it wasn't meant to be for me to have any more children. It was God's will. That made me cry even more.

I watched Joe at the counter, hoping that my ring was done. I wanted out of that store in the worst way. It was so small and cramped; besides I wanted to go back to the car and cry like a baby where no one would stare at me. Joe was headed back in my direction, but he wasn't carrying my ring alone. He had a gift bag in his hand. What did he do? And that was exactly what I said to him. "What did you do?"

He didn't say anything, and he wouldn't give me the bag until we got in the car. Once I opened the gift box, my jaw dropped. He bought one of the beautiful diamond bracelets that we were looking at. I couldn't believe it. I wanted to hug him and strangle him at the same time. When I asked him why he did it, he said he wanted to put a smile on my face. The bracelet actually serves as a memorial to the baby I never met and will never ever forget.

In the past, I never understood why women would get so upset after they miscarried. What was the big deal? It wasn't really a baby yet. Boy! Was I wrong? I felt that baby growing inside of me from the get-go. I was in a state of bereavement, not to mention having to carry the baby until the D and C was scheduled.

Off we went to the mall. I tried to put a smile on my face. I had so much to be happy about, yet I was so sad. Then I took a look at my husband Joe and my beautiful Madison and realized that everything was going to be all right. It was okay for me to be so sad, and I was going to get through it. I had the greatest support system in the world. I'm not so sure how I would've gotten through it without Maddy. She has no idea how much she helped me through the whole ordeal. She kept me going and kept me laughing with the natural innocence of a child.

The following week I went to the pre-op appointment for the D and C. It was so disturbing to me that the nurses kept referring to the procedure as an abortion. It sounded so horrible and terminal to me. I kept correcting them that it wasn't an abortion. My baby was not alive and I was not terminating the pregnancy. The nurses explained that was the term they used for D and C; they are essentially the same thing. I just hated it, but it was par for the course. It certainly was not a happy occasion, so why give it a happier title.

The procedure was pretty cut and dry. I was in and out of the hospital before I knew it. I left feeling like complete garbage, but it was final and I was no longer pregnant. Now it was time to pick up the pieces and start over. I was determined to become pregnant, so I was willing to do whatever it took to get myself better and had a year to do it. Bring on the blood tests and the birth control pills.

The first test came back, and thank God, was negative for cancer. Thankfully, all the tests came back negative. Twelve months later, I was good to go. Joe and I got the green light to start making a baby.

Enter: Evangeline Nicole

By December 2006, I was pregnant! If anything, Joey never misses. I thought it would take a few tries before I would become pregnant, but I'll take it. We were excited that we were expecting another baby, but we were extra cautious. I had to try not to become so stressed out. I certainly would not be bringing Madison to my three-month checkup. I had already taken two home pregnancy tests, so I was pretty certain that I was really carrying, but I still had to go to the doctor to confirm. Joey came with me to the first appointment, and everything was good and where it was supposed to be. Our new baby was due late October. Hoo-ha!

Of course, there would have to be a kink in the hose. A year before, I sat at the same desk and discussed my birth plan with the same doctor. Now suddenly things had changed. He knew that I was on Zoloft last time and didn't seem to have a problem with it. Now he did; he wanted me off the medication immediately. Big red light! Not good! I had been on Zoloft for four years straight; now he was going to stop me cold turkey six weeks into my pregnancy. I knew that I had discussed the medication issue with him the last time around, and my views hadn't changed since then. I told him to contact my psychiatrist; she was aware that I was pregnant and agreed that I should stay on the meds.

Now, I know that I am not a doctor, but I had educated myself enough on the medication issue. There were certain SSRI's that were safe to take while pregnant or breastfeeding and Zoloft was one of them. The benefits definitely outweighed the risks. Zoloft was associated with a very rare but serious newborn lung problem—persistent pulmonary hypertension of the newborn, or PPHN, if you take an SSRI during pregnancy; the overall risks remain extremely low. Besides, I was on the frontline doing phone support for the Resource Center. I can't tell you how many calls I would get from severely depressed mothers whose doctors had taken them off their meds, especially if the mother had a history of depression or postpartum depression. It never ended well. One of the first things a doctor tells you when taking antidepressants is *never* stop taking the medication all at once.

I was not pleased at all with my doctor. We were not on the same page, and it was very important to me that we were. What was so shocking to me was how he changed his opinion in a matter of a year. What were his reasons? I would imagine it was the legality of it all. If something happened to the baby or me, he would be held liable, I guess. But what if he took me off the meds and I became so severely depressed that I took my life or the life of my child, or even worse, I killed myself and my child? Who would be at fault then? Lord only knows what would've happened if I chose to stay with that doctor. I am confidant that it wouldn't have been good, and I was not willing to stick around to find out.

I needed to find a doctor who was educated in postpartum issues and would not be opposed to me taking meds while I was pregnant. Feeling comfortable with my doctor was very important, and I wanted to be on the same page. I definitely knew enough people in the baby making industry that would be able to help me. Within a week, I found an obstetrics and gynecology group with doctors who were familiar with the subject and a bit more current with the times. I never really cared for the larger medical groups in comparison to the exclusive care I got from one individual doctor who did not belong to a group; at this point I was willing to make exceptions. At my first appointment, I met some of the doctors in the practice, and they were all very nice. That made Joe and me very happy.

Then another miracle occurred. I got a phone call from my brother Michael, and to my surprise, he and his wife Lilly were expecting their first child. They had been married for over ten years, and I wasn't really sure if they would ever have children, although I really wanted them to. I was so happy for them. Not only were they having a baby, our babies were due right around the same time. It was fun having a pregnant partner; at all of our family functions, everyone was catering to us. We both sat back and enjoyed every minute.

This pregnancy was much different from the last two. I was not nauseous at all and didn't have any aversions or cravings for food. This time, I was thirty-five years old, so now I had to go for all these different tests to make sure there were no chromosomal abnormalities/down syndrome. That was great fun and didn't make me nervous at all. With the grace of God, everything was fine.

Surprisingly, I was fine, too (mentally). I decided in the

beginning of the pregnancy, with the approval of the psychiatrist, that I wanted to decrease the dosage of Zoloft. At that time, I was taking 150 milligrams of Zoloft; the highest possible dosage was 200 milligrams. I wanted to make sure that after I delivered the baby, I had some leeway with the medication. If I stayed on 150 milligrams throughout the pregnancy and I became severely depressed after I delivered, I would only be able to increase the dosage by 50 milligrams. I didn't want to be put in a position where I would have to change medications. The Zoloft worked very well, so I wanted to stick with that. I hear so many horror stories about these poor women who go through one medication after the next, and none of them work. I did not want to be in that position one bit. I was worried that I would become depressed or anxious with the change in dosage, but I was okay. The OCD would rear its head from time to time, but nothing too crazy. If anything, I was a little anxious about what would happen after I delivered.

At twenty weeks, I had my appointment for the ultrasound. I must admit, I was very worried; my friend the "what ifs" returned. What if the baby is missing a leg or a hand? What if the baby is not growing properly in my uterus? What if there is something wrong with the baby's heart? This time around, I was able to handle my stress and OCD thoughts a lot better. They weren't distressing me so much that I had an all-out anxiety attack. I didn't let Joe know how paranoid I was; I just kept it to myself. Initially I went in the examining room by myself; once I got the okay from the tech that everything was normal, I had Joe come in with Maddy. Now it was time to find out the sex of Baby Isnardi.

Maddy was so excited seeing the little baby that was in my stomach and its weird image on the screen. She was able to make out the arms and legs and even noticed the cute little nose. Then the tech started moving down towards the little baby hiney, and there it was, as clear as day: a little tiny vagina. We were having another girl, and this time around I was pretty confident about my new responsibilities.

We were all so happy. It was so important to me that Madison was involved with every phase of the pregnancy. I didn't want her to feel left out or like she was being replaced. For the past five years, she was number one, and I didn't want that to change for her. So Joe and I weren't having a baby; it was Madison who was having a little baby sister. We even gave her the huge responsibility of finding a name for her baby sister. It didn't take her much time because she thought of a name right away. I must admit that Joe and I were a little nervous, simply because she was five and loved SpongeBob, Shrek and Barbie dolls, but she came through like a champ. Madison's choice was Evangeline. We fell in love with it immediately, but why would a five-year-old chose such a unique name? We thought it was going to be something like Princess Magenta or Star, so we were very lucky. Evangeline was a character from the movie *Nanny McPhee* that Madison watched all the time. It was so different and just beautiful.

We took it a step further by letting Madison take charge of the baby shower and create the baby registry. Except I wasn't having a baby shower; Madison was having a baby shower for her little sister. The invitations read: "Madison is having a baby sister! Evangeline! And to celebrate the pending arrival, Grandma is throwing a baby shower for her, and you are invited to share our joy!"

Madison was overjoyed! She even got to invite some of her little girlfriends, too. It was really sweet, and Madison was the center of attention.

As for the first pregnancy, I was having a problem with

constipation. The doctor was putting me on several different kinds of pregnancy-friendly laxatives, and they weren't really working. I was eating fruits and vegetables and drinking plenty of water, but it didn't make much of difference. I was still having a very hard time moving my bowels. I really didn't think that it was such a big deal until the day it became a really big problem.

I would attempt to go to the bathroom and sit for thirty minutes at a time, and nothing would happen. One afternoon I was in so much pain. My stomach hurt really badly, so I decided to call the OB. The doctor told me to try some prune juice and try to go for short walks. I couldn't stand up straight, let alone go for short walks, but I did as I was told. An hour went by, and nothing happened. I would pass a little bit of stool, but there was something much bigger that wanted to come out. It was an all too familiar feeling. I called the doctor's office back after two hours of prune juice and agonizing pain, and they told me to go to the hospital. So off we went, Joe and I, rushing to the hospital because I couldn't shit. Again, I was sitting backwards in the seat because my ass hurt.

We were there for a few hours, and nothing was happening. I was so uncomfortable, not to mention the different straps and wires all around my belly and arms. Finally, one of the doctors arrived, and had the nurse give me a laxative. Thirty minutes later, it was smooth sailing, and I was able to go home.

As for the birth, the doctors decided that I should have a C-section because I had so much difficulty giving birth to Madison. I was a little disappointed because I wanted to try a natural childbirth, but I didn't want to take any chances. The date was set for October 23rd; at least I knew exactly when she was coming. About two weeks later after my date was set, I found out that my brother and sister-in-law were having a scheduled C-section as well. They went for the sonogram and found out they were having a baby boy. Kyle Andrew was set to arrive on October 26th. It was a truly a miracle. We couldn't have planned that if we tried.

Then it happened again. I couldn't go to the bathroom. I wanted to, but nothing was coming out. Same old nonsense, except this time I was getting contractions, and I was only thirty weeks pregnant. I started the back and forth nonsense on the phone with the doctor. This particular doctor wanted me to try glycerin suppositories because the stool softeners were not working. Nothing happened, just more cramping and pain. Back to the hospital we went at 6:00 p.m. with me sitting backwards in the front seat. It was beyond ridiculous at this stage of the game.

Hours went by as I lay on my side once again with straps and monitors all over my body. I was so uncomfortable and irritated. I had impacted stool once again. All I needed was someone to stick their finger in my ass like Dr. Jean did five years before, but for whatever reason, these doctors just didn't get it. Instead they kept giving me laxatives that were doing nothing. I was crying because I was in so much pain.

After five hours of begging the nurses, one of my doctors decides to show up at 11:00 p.m. They couldn't do anything for me except give me laxatives until he showed his stupid face. So there he was Dr. X, in all of his glory. He told me he couldn't help me; all that he could do was give me the laxatives. I wanted to jump out of the bed and strangle him, but I couldn't because I was strapped down by all of the damn wires that were connected to my body. I drank so much of the laxative they gave me that I literally started throwing up as soon as it went down my throat, and now he wanted to give me more. I screamed at him. "Are you kidding me? You can't give me any more laxatives; it is obviously not working!"

"What would you like me to do? You are constipated, and all that I can give you is the laxative."

"You're the fucking doctor here, not me. I am not constipated, I have impacted stool There is obviously a blockage of some kind. I have been through this before. I just can't believe that you can't figure it out! I refuse to take any more damn laxatives! I have thrown it up twice already!"

He looked scared and speechless. I was crying hysterically and shaking. Joey was just standing by my side, holding my hand and shaking his head. This was not my idea of a stress-free pregnancy.

"I am going to have to call in a gastroenterologist and have you scheduled for a sonogram to make sure everything is okay with the baby as a precautionary measure. Try to relax and the gastro doctor will be here shortly," Dr. X said.

Try to relax! Sure! That was easy for him to say. Joey stayed as long as they would allow him until he got thrown out at 1:00 a.m. I was so scared, and I didn't want him to leave me, but he had no choice. Was I going to lose my baby again? I was so close. I didn't know how I would recover from this if I lost this baby. Somehow I managed to fall asleep, even though I was a restless mess. At 3:00 a.m., the nurses abruptly awakened me. I was having contractions, and that wasn't good. They had to administer medication to stop the contractions. Once again, I felt like the baby was going to come out of my asshole.

They woke me again at 6:00 a.m. to go for the sonogram, and by that time, Joey was back, and I was thrilled to see him. After the sonogram, they kept trying to give me the same damn laxative that they were giving me all day before. I refused to take it because all it did was make me throw up. Right after breakfast, the gastroenterologist came, and he got right down to business. He asked me a few questions, then put his gloves on and shoved his hand up my ass. "You have an impacted stool!"

No kidding!

"You are not constipated. Why were they giving you so many laxatives? You are completely blocked up!"

Finally! A competent doctor. Thank you Lord!

Within minutes, he had the nurses prepping me for an enema. Guess what? It worked right away. It was just like magic. I was furious at the OB. This whole episode could've been avoided if I had a competent doctor who actually listened to me. What is even scarier? These are the doctors that I chose to deliver my baby. I was so close to my due date that it wasn't worth switching doctors, yet again. I just requested that I had no more interactions with Dr. X.

Stress-free was how I really tried to live my life, but it was very short-lived. My mother has always been at my beck and call, and then that changed too. My grandmother came to stay with my parents for a few months until she was able to move into her new home. That meant that my mother had to tend to my eighty-three-year-old grandmother, which I am sure was not easy. My grandma is a very active lady and needs to be entertained at all times. I truly needed my mother's help as I grew bigger and bigger, not to mention that I am a total mommy's girl. If I wasn't with her, I was on the phone with her, and that was just the way it was. Now I had to share her, and that was a lot for me to get used to. It really stressed me out.

I guess living all day and night with the same person takes a toll on a relationship, especially when you haven't lived with that person for 40 years. My mother and grandmother fought constantly about everything, and now I had two mothers giving me their opinions and telling me what to do. Let's not forget Madison, she had her opinions too; she fought with all of us. It was a nightmare.

In September, Madison started kindergarten in a new school, and she loved it. We were so afraid she wouldn't like her new environment because the preschool she attended was like a cult. At the orientation, it seemed like a wonderful place, but boy we were wrong. Madison hated her preschool and never wanted to go. She would undress herself in the backseat of the car before we got to school. When we would arrive at the school, she would be stark naked in her car seat, crying her eyes out. It was like a torture chamber to her; my heart would break every day that I dropped her off. The Pre-K school she was in wasn't affiliated with the new school; we definitely did our homework researching a new school for her this time around. This new school was a highly recommended Catholic School that was extremely family-oriented. I was just worried that she would have a problem adjusting to the full day of school, but she was fine. She started making friends right away and wanted to go.

By the beginning of October I was ready and couldn't wait to have Evangeline. This pregnancy had gone by so much quicker than I thought it would. I know I had my problems medically, but everything seemed to be getting better. I had only gained about 25 pounds this time around, so she was a lot easier to carry. I had made it through most of the pregnancy, and so far, no depression. I started to get anxious and worried because I was having her on October 23rd; "what if" the medication doesn't work after I deliver? What happens next? I started calling all of my Postpartum Resource Center friends for guidance. Some of the moms didn't go through PPD the second time around, so it was really important that I kept in touch when them. They were all so wonderful and helped put me at ease, for the moment.

My mom, my grandmother and I decided to take Madison pumpkin picking on the east end of Long Island; it was getting closer to Halloween, and I wasn't sure if I or Joe would have time to take her after the baby was born. It was a lot fun watching Maddy pick pumpkins and run through the cornfields, even though my mother and grandmother were at each other's throats. My mother got a phone call from my stepfather's job; Vito had a stroke! The fun ended really quickly after that phone call.

We tried to rush home. We were all the way toward the east end of Long Island. Vito worked in Nassau County, which was West, closer to New York City. We had no idea that Vito drove himself home from work. We thought someone from work was driving him to the hospital or driving him home. By the time we got to Mother's house, he was already there. The plus side is that he was alive, but he was slurring his words and had limited feeling in both of his legs. My mother begged him to go to the hospital, but he refused. He didn't think he was having a stroke; he was prescribed new allergy meds the day before, so he figured it was a side effect. Besides, he had work the next day and had to go! At 4:30 a.m., Vito woke up and asked my mother to take him to the hospital. Once there, the doctors told my mother that he had suffered several strokes and should have been admitted to a hospital days before. By that time he could barely speak, had no feeling in either leg at all and limited use of his hands. Vito would not be going to work the next day. He wouldn't be going back to work again.

Now it was a week before I was going to deliver Evangeline, my stepfather was in the hospital recovering from multiple strokes, and my mother was on the verge of a nervous breakdown. Let's not forget my grandmother, who didn't want to be with any of us; she wanted to be home. Not only was I delivering, but my brother and Lilly were delivering their baby three days after I was as well. Not good!

I felt so bad for my mother. She was being pulled in so many different directions that her head was spinning out of control. Vito, Mike and Lilly, and Joe and I were all going to be at different hospitals nowhere near each other all at the same time. It was becoming increasingly problematic for me, too, because I needed my mom to watch Madison while I was in the hospital delivering Evangeline. Madison was extremely attached to my mother and didn't want to be with anyone else.

My house of cards was falling apart really fast along with my sanity. I was feeling so stressed out about being stressed out. Luckily, Vito was going to be okay; he just needed a lot of rehabilitation with his memory, leg and arm function. I was feeling sorry that I wouldn't be at the hospital when Michael and Lilly were delivering Kyle, but it was beyond my control. I wanted to help my mother as well, but I was powerless. I had to stay focused and not let all of the stress get the best of me. I started going for prenatal massages, and it did wonders for stress level. For an hour every week, I would release all of my worries and try to regroup.

Everything worked itself out, and on October 23rd, all the pieces fell into place. I woke up at 4:30 a.m., ready to have a baby. Maddy slept in bed with Joe and me that night, and I hugged her all night long. After that day, Maddy would no longer be an only child; she was going to be a big sister. I stared at her as she slept in bed, and I started to cry. I brought myself back to that horrible place I was in five years earlier and remembered the hell I went through. I was feeling apprehensive because I was afraid that upon my return home, I could possibly revisit that hell. Madison was five years old and as sharp as a knife; she would pick up my depressed mood right away. I couldn't put her through that.

My mother came to my house at 5:00 a.m.; she was going to

stay with Maddy and take her to school that morning. That gave her the freedom she needed to run back and forth to all the different hospitals and tend to my grandmother.

We arrived at the maternity center, and the staff was ready for us. I was in my own special caesarian section birthing room, where I spent a good portion of the morning prepping for the surgery. It was a much more relaxed atmosphere from my last birthing experience to say the very least. Joe sat with me, and I didn't throw up on him like I did last time. We relaxed, watched television and talked about everything. What was this little girl going to be like? Who would she look like? She definitely had some tough competition because Madison was absolutely perfect in every way. We thought about her a lot, and I wished that she was there with us. I missed my Maddy.

Then, it was my turn to go in! I was so scared to go and wanted Joe to come with me, but he couldn't. As the nurses pushed my bed out of the room, I closed my eyes and silently prayed to God. "Please let everything be okay. Please help my baby and make sure that she is healthy. And *please* don't let me get sick again. Please don't let me slip through into Hell because I don't think I could live through it this time!" I opened my eyes, and I couldn't control my tears. I was petrified. The nurse grabbed my hand and told me that everything was going to be okay. She had such sincerity in her voice that I believed her for the moment.

The operating room was freezing cold, bright and filled with people. It was time to leave the cozy warm hospital bed and hop on the sub-zero operating table. Of course they had to remove my robe, so I was stark naked, cold and everything was hanging out all over the place. Thank goodness the nurses shaved me ahead of time. Then something wonderful happened; they put a heated blanket on me, and it was fabulous! I was actually feeling quite relaxed as they strapped wires and Velcro cuffs on my legs and my body. The OB and anesthesiologist came dressed in their scrubs, ready for business; it was baby time. The quick transition from consciousness to unconsciousness was amazing to me. One minute I was wide awake, and then the anesthesiologist asked me to count backwards from ten, and I don't think I made it past eight. I was out! I tried to get a last minute prayer in, but that never happened. I felt nothing at all; I was sound asleep.

Then I was awake again, and Joe was standing right next to me with this beautiful little angel; Evangeline Nicole was finally here, and she was just perfect. She was six pounds thirteen ounces and nineteen and a half inches long with a perfectly round head. I looked her over to make sure all of her fingers and toes were accounted for, and she was flawless. Joey stood by my side as I cried, watching the nurses clean her and wrap her up like a pea in a pod. Joey put Evangeline right next to my face, and she smelled unbelievable. I was in love all over again, but I was so afraid. I didn't have time to wipe my tears off of my face because I was out like a light, again.

I woke up in my room, and my whole family was there, including my little Madison. Evangeline was sleeping in her little bassinet, unaware of all the hubbub going on around her. I was so happy to see Madison, and she was equally happy to see me. She seemed amazed by Evangeline, not truly understanding how the baby got here. She felt my stomach and asked how they got her out, so I told her the truth; the doctors opened up my stomach, took her out, then closed me up. I had the scar to prove it. That was a lot easier than telling her about the "other" place babies come out of.

I was feeling very tired and wanted to go back to sleep, but most of all, I was okay. I was a bit anxious, but I wasn't hearing any voices or seeing things that weren't there, and wasn't feeling paranoid or detached. I felt pretty good and that was great.

After all the visitors left for the day, it was just Joe, Maddy, Evangeline, and me: the new family. I had the room all to myself, no roommate. I wasn't able to keep Evangeline in the room because I couldn't get out of the bed if I had to tend to her. That was okay with me too; I wanted to get as much sleep as possible. Plus they were giving me Benadryl and pain medication, so I was ready for a nice peaceful sleep.

They woke me at 7:00 a.m. to eat breakfast and give me my meds. I was going to have the morning to Evangeline and myself. Joey was chaperoning a field trip at Maddy's school, and my mother was going to the hospital to visit my stepfather. I wouldn't have any visitors until later on in the afternoon. I was feeling anxious and worried; I felt like there was a black cloud trying to push its way over my head, and I was doing everything to avoid it.

The nurses wanted me up, and walking that morning and this time around it was much easier than when I had delivered Madison. After that, I was given the okay to take care of Evangeline for the day. It was awkward at first; the last time I held a baby so small and new to the world, it was Madison. Evangeline seemed much more fragile than Madison. Evangeline had a pinkish color to her skin and a perfect little face, just like her sister. I fell in love with her just as quickly as I did with Madison. I never really had the chance to have any one-on-one time with Madison when we were in the hospital, simply because I always had either my husband or mother there with me. I enjoyed every second with her, just staring at her as I fed her. Then she opened her eyes, and I saw that they were a beautiful shade of gray; it was amazing. She stayed with me for lunch; I changed her diaper and watched her sleep. I felt a little bit anxious, but I was good. So far, no psychosis or severe depression.

My peaceful Mommy/Evangeline time came to a screeching halt when my new roommate surfaced. She had a huge family that spoke really freaking loud, and they stayed until they got thrown out. They were so obnoxious and had no regard for me at all. Joey and Madison showed up at 2:30 p.m., right after Madison's field trip. We had a great afternoon together and took a whole bunch of pictures of Madison and Evangeline. Madison fed her a bottle; seeing her interact with her new little sister was unbelievable. I was so proud; Madison was so mature and caring for a five-year-old. We had a huge love festival going on, and it was awesome, but I still felt that black cloud looming around me.

I had many visitors coming in and out all night. I was so tired and couldn't wait to go to sleep, so I decided to have Evangeline sleep in the nursery. One thing I remember that is so important to new moms is sleep, uninterrupted, peaceful sleep. I didn't feel guilty about it this time around either. Joe and Madison left at 9:30 p.m., when the nurses came in to give me my pain meds. I assumed that my new roommate's guests would follow suit, but I was wrong. They stayed until midnight and spoke this annoying language that I have never heard before. They were from another planet or something, and they were so damn loud. Finally the nurses insisted that they leave. Ah, I could close my eyes and go to sleep. Not so! This girl had a deviated septum or something, because she snored loud; I wanted to gag her. Not only did she snore, but she was an extremely sound sleeper. She decided to have her baby sleep with her, but she wouldn't wake when the baby cried. I must have called the nurses into the room three times that night, and finally they brought her baby into the nursery. I was not a happy girl, and that made me anxious.

The next day, Michael and Lilly came to visit before she was due to go to the hospital and deliver baby Kyle; I was so upset that

Enter: Evangeline Nicole

I wasn't going to be there for the birth, but there was truly nothing I could do about it, and that made me anxious too. I had a ton of anxiety, and that made me even more anxious. I had to chill out and stop worrying so much; it was detrimental to my being.

Another sleepless night with my roommate, her rude family, and her crazy snoring. Thank God it was her last night because she had a natural childbirth, so she would get booted out of the hospital the next day. The following night, I got a wonderful, roommate-less, drug-induced sleep.

Kyle Andrew, my first nephew, was born on October 26th, beautiful and healthy. Two miracles in one week. We couldn't have planned this if we tried. I couldn't wait to finally meet him. My last day in the hospital was on a very hot and humid Saturday afternoon. I was extra, extra anxious that day. I was okay in the hospital, but what was going to happen when I got home? Joey and Madison were there early that morning. At this stage in my life, my home was bigger, and now I had four dogs: two German Shepherds, one Jack Russell Terrier and my love, Petey-Dog, who was around for the first birth. According to my mother, the house was a complete mess. I felt so bad for my mother because she was all over the place, visiting different hospitals with my grandmother in tow. She was visibly exhausted when I saw her the night before, but she insisted on being at my house that day to clean up and help me out. I needed her to be 100 percent, God forbid "it" happened to me again, and at this point, she was about 25 percent. That wasn't good.

While we waited for the discharge papers, there were screams coming from the room directly across from mine. My heart automatically dropped to the floor. I walked out to see what was going on, and I was pushed back into my room. Doctors and nurses were rushing into the room in a panic. I was freaking out. What was going on in there? The patient's family members were running around crying, and I couldn't make out what they were saying because they were speaking another language. I automatically assumed that something happened to her as a result of PPD or psychosis. Did she attempt kill herself or the baby in the hospital?

After fifteen minutes of panic, a nurse came in to tell us what was going on. Apparently the new mom thought she was having a heart attack, but it turned out she didn't. I knew what happened. That poor mother was probably petrified and had a full blown anxiety attack. That little setback did not help my condition at all. The black cloud was still looming around my head.

We were discharged and sent on our way home. I had the same bizarre emotions that I did with Madison as we left the hospital, crying because one day Evangeline would no longer love or need me. Other than that, it was an extremely uneventful ride home, but I remember it being really humid and unseasonably warm outside. Joey drove as slow as a snail, and I appreciated his pace. Madison had so many questions about her new little sister; it was kind of cute that she was so intrigued by her.

When we arrived at our house, I had this strange feeling of hesitation and fear. I didn't want to get out of the car. Was it going to happen to me again? If it did, was I going to be strong enough to handle it? I was truly terrified, but I was trying to hide it as best as I could.

My mother was there with my grandmother trying to tidy up, but the house was still a disaster area. There was only so much my mother could do with her limited schedule; I was just truly happy to see her. She was only able to stay for an hour or so because she had to run off to see my brother and Lilly at one hospital, then Vito, at another. She looked completely frazzled and on edge. I wished there was something more I could do for her, but my hands were completely tied. I needed to be strong and help myself at this point.

I settled in with Evangeline and got everything set up in my bedroom for her. She would be sharing the room with Joe and me until she was old enough to stay in her own room. As I got her bassinet ready, I sat on my bed and stared off into the distance, remembering Madison in that same bassinet. I remembered the hell that I went through and how badly I wanted to remove myself from everything and everyone. I put my hands on my face to wipe my tears and prayed to God again to help me. "God please don't let this happen to me again! Please help me!"

Joey knew how important it was for me to get as much sleep as possible, so he sent me up to our room early to get some sleep. He was well aware of how scared I was and did everything he could to help me. I love him dearly for that. Joe is such an exceptional father, and he accepted the role like a natural; my mind was completely at ease because I knew how capable he was.

I got the sleep that I needed, but life had much more in store for me. Evangeline loved to cry, and boy did she have a set of lungs on her! She cried for hours all day and night, and as my luck would have it, Evangeline had colic! We tried everything, gas drops, brine water, special swaddling sleepers and nothing worked. So Joe and I started sleeping in shifts; it was the only way that we could both get some form of sleep. Evangeline cried so much and so loud that she would wake up Madison, who was sleeping in her own room. Our end result: Joe, Evangeline, Madison, all four dogs and myself were all sleeping in the same room. For the most part, none of us slept.

With all of my sleep issues and frazzled nerves, I was just waiting for the depression storm to come over me. I was questioning myself on whether or not I was depressed. I certainly didn't feel as bad as I did the first time, but I had only been home from the hospital two weeks, and my crushing suicidal depression didn't start until my third week home with Madison. I started calling all of my PPD friends, asking crazy questions about how they felt the second time around, and they all said the same thing: a paranoid mess, waiting for the bottom to fall out. And that was how I felt. I was just waiting for it to happen; I was a sitting duck.

The situation at my mother's house was getting worse by the second. My stepfather was home from the hospital, but as a result of the stroke, he became extremely depressed. He would actually sit around and cry about nothing. It was a very sad situation, and I really felt bad for my mother. This should have been one of the happiest times in her life; I had another baby, and Michael and Lilly had their first child. Grandmothers live for that stuff, but she couldn't enjoy it the way she wanted to. The atmosphere at her house was detrimental to my well-being. As soon as I walked into the house, I felt the happiness being sucked right out of my body, so I avoided going there at all costs.

One afternoon, I took my mother, Vito (who was crying), my grandmother, Evangeline and Madison to Mike and Lilly's house so we could finally meet my beautiful nephew, Kyle. He was perfect in every way. My brother and Lilly fell into the role of mommy and daddy very quickly, and they were good at it. Madison was the big sister and older cousin, just like that. She used to be the only one; she was the baby, but she loved her new job of helping out, getting diapers and bottles.

Over time, everything started falling into place; my stepfather was feeling better and going to physical therapy. After a few months, Evangeline's colic went away, my grandmother finally moved into her new home, and my mother was back to her normal, happy, helpful self once again. As for me, nothing happened. I was fine; I was better than fine, I was extraordinarily happy. I was the proud mother of two beautiful girls. I finally knew what it was like to have a newborn and be completely happy. Along with the happiness came the guilt; how I wished that I didn't suffer so badly with Madison, because those first months of motherhood were magical.

My Wife (For Men's Eyes Only)

Written by Joseph Isnardi

I remember the first time I saw my wife many years ago. I just recall seeing this girl walking into my workplace looking for her brother. I'm not going to lie here: she was good looking, and I wanted to have sex with her regardless of whether or not she was crazy. As with most men, I was attracted to her physically, and the emotional part wouldn't come 'til later. But when it came, it never left, even throughout this entire ordeal that most people take for granted. Pregnancy and childbirth are wonderful events in a person's life, but it didn't seem too wonderful at the time.

I want to start off by saying I'm a guy. I am not incredibly corny or overly emotional. You're not going to see me cry or get much compassion from me, but what I can say is that PPD is a real condition, and it's not just in a woman's mind. Before all that, let's get started on my wife and how this whole mess came to be.

Wendy actually started working at the car dealership where I worked, doing some kind of office work while I washed cars in the back. Every so often, she'd come to the back of the shop, and I would incessantly hit on her. One big problem though: she was married. But I couldn't be deterred. Besides, if you saw her husband, you'd figure anyone had some sort of sporting chance. So basically, I would see her every day and make some sort of attempt at hitting on her. I thought it was working, considering it took a few years. I'd have to say, it was working slowly.

After all those years, I figured I'd try something different, so I ignored her. Everyone told me there was no chance for me and that I shouldn't bother. But I was twenty-one years old and pretty much as horny as possible, so what did I have to lose.

I noticed that after a few days of keeping my distance, she started seeking me out. It was pretty much a typical guy move, but back in my day, I didn't think women were too hard to figure out. In some aspects, I am right, in others I am way off. Once she started looking for me, I decided it was time to ask her how she felt about me. Another bold move in the series of events, but hey, it was all working so far.

Wendy denied liking me, of course, but we both knew she was full of it. As I figured, she seemed receptive to the whole thing, so I went even further and told her that she kept checking out my ass whenever I would walk by. No outright denial there. I was all but in, and to add to my odds, she was recently separated from her husband! This flirting kept on going for a little while, and quite frankly, I can't remember how long. All I recall is walking outside of our workplace with her, or sort of following her. I guess it depends on whose version you like, and I like mine much better. So there we were; she got into her truck, and I stood outside of the driver's door. I am not sure what I was thinking, but I am sure it wasn't children, a house, marriage and car payments. It's a pretty safe bet it was something much more immediate and much more gratifying at twenty-one years old. So I literally went in head first and hoped for the best. Well, it worked; we kissed. I knew I could do it. That was the beginning; everything changed from that moment forward.

Since I am writing this chapter for the guys with wives who are going through or have gone through PPD, I am not going to go into intricate details of a love affair or some sappy crap like that. Let's just say after a couple weeks, she was chasing me, and in the meantime, she was also in the middle of a divorce. Wendy has a much different version of events; mine is just a little bit more candid. But the end result was the same: I loved her, and she loved me, and we were in the midst of a relationship.

And that was when I realized how much of a pain the OCD was, but hey, they're all nuts in some way, right? The first problem with OCD was the fact that Wendy could not let anything go. She just held on to things like a pit bull. Tell me if this makes any sense: everything I did and every way I acted is what drew her to me, yet was exactly everything she complained about. When we first got together, she just couldn't get over my past. She was questioning everything I did, who I slept with, who I dated and why. I assumed she just wasn't able to get the picture of me with someone else out of her head. Wendy claims that she has only had sex with a few people; I didn't believe her at first, but her story hasn't changed in eight and a half years. She never understood how I could have sex with someone who I wasn't in love with.

Before I continue on with the negative aspects of OCD, let me just say that I love her dearly, and through it all, I wouldn't change a thing. But since she's kind of making me do this, I get to vent about her OCD, and she is not allowed to get mad.

Wendy couldn't stop the OCD thoughts from running through her head. So if she had a bad thought about me, she was stuck with it. I saw a trend in her that made me wonder if our relationship would work. Whenever I would go out without her or do anything that didn't involve her, she would playfully tell me to have a good time. But when I got home, I'd get a ton of shit for it. It would never be about me going out, but somehow I did something to piss her off when I was gone. For instance, I didn't call enough, or I was late, or I came home and ignored her, or she would have some other negative reaction when I would walk through the door. This was Wendy's way of making me stay home without saying it.

So I couldn't call her a "bad" girlfriend because she could say "I never have a problem with you going out. It's all in your head." Bullshit! We both knew the truth. She ran some kind of scenario in her head all night repeatedly and drove herself nuts. It could be me dying on the side of the road in some fiery crash or running off with some other woman. I wish when I was single that I had half the luck with women she always thought I did.

Another thing about OCD was that she always thought she had burned the house down whenever we left to go somewhere. My wife always left three things on in the house: the curling iron, the clothes iron and the stove. I wish I could get reimbursed for every mile I put on my car driving back to the house to make sure they were turned off.

I'm sure you get the idea about her condition. If you are reading this, I am sure that you've dealt with it in one form or another, or maybe you're even dealing with it now. I know I sound miserable. Well I put it all this way to show you that it can all be changed.

If you are at your wits end, don't throw in the towel just yet. The woman you fell in love with is there, and with a little work and some medication, she will be back for good. My wife is my world, and for every *down* associated with OCD, there is an _up_. Actually, there is a way up!

In October of 2001, we bought a house, and one week later, we found out Wendy was pregnant. I am not going to say I was thrilled. I was scared shitless. I'd never really been around kids, I didn't know a lot about them, and certainly never thought about having them either. I knew one day it would happen, just not so soon. So I put a brave face on and started getting ready to have a baby.

Now it's time for me to take some of the blame for my part in making Wendy's OCD much worse. I've said my wife is my world, and my daughters are everything in it, but I am not the type of person who thinks that pregnant women are glowing and beautiful. I watched my wife grow day by day and knew it wasn't permanent, but I acted as if it was. I know I was wrong, and next time around, I will be better, but I will never think it's sexy or attractive. Just remember that if you want things to get better, you have to help your loved ones along. No one is going to change for you if you can't appreciate who they are and what they become in the first place. So Wendy became insecure, and I didn't do much to help it change for the better. There is my blame; I accept it and do feel guilty as hell about it.

July 15, 2002, we are in the hospital, and Wendy was about to give birth to our daughter. That's when my baby's heart rate dropped, and they pulled my wife away from me and took her into the operating room. I did not appreciate my child coming into the world until I thought I was about to lose her. These were the first tears I had shed in a very long time.

I won't rehash that moment since I am sure Wendy explained it fully, but this was where the PPD began. When you think spending five minutes with the possibility of losing your newborn is heart wrenching, try extending that horror for a few more months watching your wife spiral down, becoming a stranger you never thought she'd be.

I remember Wendy telling me she was feeling kind of sad. I didn't give it much thought. I just thought she was being a "woman." I wish I could've stopped it there, I really do. I don't have vivid details of this time because it wasn't happening to me. I guess that is my point to every guy reading this: "*It is not happening to you!*" You cannot think for a second you have any idea what a woman is going through with this. My wife went from laughing almost every minute of the day to the point that I wanted to strangle her for being so happy, then she became a lifeless, crying, depressed mess that lay in bed all day. Wendy disappeared totally, and I had no idea why.

Wendy told me that it was postpartum depression. I had heard of it before, but like most men, I thought it was a crock of shit. I didn't know if she just got lazy or didn't care anymore, and I began to resent the shit out of her for it. She dragged me through a pregnancy and childbirth that I was scared enough about, and now she was abandoning me to care for this little baby without any help. Once again, I just didn't get it.

Other guys in this situation are no help whatsoever. If you remember one thing about this chapter please let it be this: *don't, I repeat, don't listen to a single thing any guy friend of yours has to say about it!* They are probably more clueless than you, and everything they tell you will pretty much reinforce every stereotype and negative connotation associated with it. Friends will tell you that your wife is full of shit and is lazy, or she just doesn't want to get up at night and is sticking you with it. And my all time favorite: "It is all in her head."

If your wife was that type of woman, you would have known it long before this. No woman you would fall in love with who would want to have a baby so badly would start acting like this. She is not playing some sort of game to avoid her newborn. She is very sick and needs help.

I have a lot of guilt about this time because, just like every other guy, I thought it was about me. Why is my wife ignoring my child and me? I got very angry. I recall coming home from work every day and seeing my mother-in-law with Madison while Wendy was lying in bed. My blood would boil when I had to hear all the new things Madison was doing from my mother-in-law and not from Wendy. I wanted to hear it from the mother of my child.

Wendy dragged me to her therapist with her. I didn't want to go. I said to myself, "this is psycho-babble bullshit, and I wish she would just get over it already!"

After a few weeks, my anger turned into fear. I was scared for her life; this was not the woman I married. Maybe this isn't in her head; it has to be something more, something way beyond what I could understand. She was sick, and when you are sick, you need medical help, not a husband who is going to make you feel worse.

I joke with Wendy now about some things during this period. One thing I always tell her is when she was going through PPD, it was the first time she ever shut up, and I actually enjoyed it. That was true for about a day, and then I missed everything about her and desperately wanted her back.

Well she came back with the help of a lot of people, whom I thank to this day. All the doctors and therapists did wonders for her, and they really were her angels. It took a lot of time and patience.

Just remember, if your wife had cancer or any other disease, you wouldn't expect her to be better in a day, so don't expect that in this situation either. Just know that it will get better, and don't forget that.

Here's the best part of it all. Not only did she recover from PPD, but she really turned her OCD around too. I know I mentioned how miserable I sounded at the beginning of all this, but I wanted to prove a point. Things are better than ever. The insecurity has gone, the thoughts have subsided, the woman I first met is back, and I am certain she is here to stay . . .

After Evangeline was born, I was scared out of my mind; I knew we would get through whatever nightmare would be bestowed upon us, but I was dreading what was about to come. Evangeline arrived, healthy and screaming her head off. I can remember just telling myself, *I need to let my wife sleep.* I recalled her telling me that getting sleep was extremely important in recovering from the birth and avoiding PPD. I am sure there is much more to it, but I will be honest: I only listen to half of what people say sometimes. So I just stuck to that philosophy of letting her sleep. I made her go to bed every night, and I stayed up with our little tyrant. Each day I got up and waited for my wife to say "It's back!" Then the ordeal would start all over again. I watched her every expression, every mood swing, every twitch in her face that might mean she had PPD again. In an extremely fortunate turn of events, each day passed and the old memories faded away. That monster who overcame our lives so many years ago didn't return. My little Evangeline is a bundle of torture and joy to this day. Most people say she is exactly like me, which for me is a scary thought. She screams, she yells, she laughs, she cries, and most of all, she loves to just be herself.

One last thought: every so often, her OCD can pop up and rear its ugly head, but hell, I am no angel either.

Through a Mother's Eyes: Wendy's Mommy

Written by Patricia Guttilla

J uly 15, 2002 at 5:45 a.m. my phone rang, and it was Wendy. "Mom, Joey is bringing me to the hospital now. I am in labor. Meet us there."

And I was on my way. I was washed, dressed and in the birthing room by 6:10 a.m.

This was the happiest day of my life. My only daughter was going to have her first baby. My baby was going to have a baby. My first grandchild. Love, joy, excitement and pride filled my body. Little did I know that within the next few months, I would go through the full spectrum of emotions any human being could experience.

I completed Lamaze training with Wendy and Joey, so I was able to join them in the birthing room. I was so proud that they both wanted me to be there with them to experience this miracle. I was shocked to see how well my daughter was doing during the labor. She did everything right, never screaming in pain.

Suddenly things seemed to be going wrong. Wendy had monitors hooked up to her, constantly checking the vitals of both her and the baby. Wendy began to go into labor. The nurses instructed her to roll over on her right side and then on her left. This seemed to go on forever. The last straw was when they made her roll over onto all fours. I was becoming very concerned; I didn't understand what was going on. We were informed the baby's heart rate was down. Actually, the baby was squeezing the umbilical cord, cutting off her own oxygen.

Within seconds, a dozen doctors and nurses were in the room. They were prepping Wendy for surgery. Scrambling around her, they pushed her into the operating room. I was frightened, but I didn't want to alarm Joey. I put my arms around him, and we just hugged. I believed he was as frightened as I was.

A nurse came out of the operating room handing Joey scrubs. "They're too tight Mom," he said.

I looked at him and shook my head. "Just go. Get in there; she needs you." I didn't give him a chance to answer as I gently shoved him out.

The time I spent alone was a nightmare. I didn't know what was happening. Was my daughter okay? Was the baby okay? Was I going to lose my daughter or the baby? Suddenly I heard a baby cry. I knew the baby was born, but was she all right? And how was my daughter? Was she all right? Was she alive? I had no idea.

Within seconds, Joey came into the room with the miracle bundle. Madison was perfect. Every feature was magnificent. On her head was the most adorable knitted pink hat. I was in awe, almost in a trance staring at her. Joey told me Wendy was all right. She had an emergency caesarian section. Wendy was wheeled out of the operating room in a complete daze. I leaned over and kissed her gently on the cheek. I was so thankful God didn't take her or Madison from me that day. I was so blessed.

The next few days in the hospital, I watched Wendy and Joey take care of Madison. They were such good parents, so gentle and loving. Both fed and changed her with ease. I was so proud. After being in the hospital for a week, Wendy and Madison came home. Wendy was a little sore; however, that didn't keep her down. She was right by her baby's side. The joint parenting continued; Joey fed and changed Madison just as much as Wendy did.

One day, I asked Joey how Wendy was doing. I asked him if he noticed her crying or sad. I asked this because I was a little blue after the birth of my children. I remember crying a little and not wanting to be alone. I remember my mother referring to this as the baby blues or melancholy. Joey told me she was fine; he didn't notice any changes in her behavior.

I spent the next few weeks helping Wendy with the baby. Due to the caesarian surgery, she was restricted from some activities. I would stay the nights that Joey worked late. One evening, Wendy and I had dinner and watched the movie, *The Others*. In the middle of the movie, Wendy became very agitated. She told me she didn't feel well and needed to go to sleep. I didn't think anything of it at the time. I felt it was good for her to take advantage of the fact that I was there and she should try to get some sleep.

Wendy called me the next day telling me that she wasn't feeling like herself. She demanded that I come to her house Monday morning before Joey left for work because she didn't want to be alone. I spoke with her several times, and each time, she was even more upset than the next.

This was the beginning of a nightmare. I arrived at her house at

6:45 a.m. as Joey left for work. Wendy called her doctor to schedule an appointment. However, she wasn't satisfied with knowing she had an appointment with her doctor. Wendy wanted immediate help. She was crying inconsolably. I held her on my lap, rocking her back and forth, hugging her. She was totally engulfed by the fear of what was happening to her. "Mom I should be so happy, I have a wonderful husband and a beautiful daughter, and look at me. I am miserable."

When Joey got home from work that day, Wendy sat us both down in the living room. Wendy started crying unstoppably. She was telling Joey and me that she wanted to go back to the hospital so she could rest. She said she was overwhelmed, exhausted and confused with her feelings. All she could do was cry—well, not cry; sob was more like it.

I looked at Joey, and he looked at me. Without saying a word to each other, I believe we both knew what the other was thinking. If we took her back to the hospital and told them how she was acting and what she was saying, they would commit her. We tried to convince her going back to the hospital to rest was not the answer. Joey had suggested that she see a psychiatrist.

Some details are a little fuzzy now, thank God. What I do remember is that Wendy called everyone she knew. She called friends, family, her friend's moms and anyone else she could think of, asking if they could shed some light on what was happening to her. I felt it was definitely related to having the baby. After a few days, I realized that it was a bit more than the baby blues. It was much more than that.

Wendy contacted a therapist from her medical plan. The appointment with that therapist was a disaster. Meanwhile, Joey and I did not leave her alone. She was afraid to feed, dress or bathe Madison. She was telling me that she was afraid Madison's neck

240

would snap while she was dressing her. Wendy had a constant gaze in her eyes instead of the beaming glow she had in her eyes a week earlier. I was extremely worried about Wendy, Joey and Madison. There were times when Wendy cried on my shoulder, and I was crying too. I was just as frightened as she was.

Miraculously, she met her Lamaze instructor one day while she was with Joey and Madison. That was the day her recovery began. Her Lamaze instructor got her in touch with a therapist and with Sonia of the Postpartum Resource Center. It was definitely not smooth sailing from there. Wendy had a very long road ahead of her. I remember going to her house in the mornings before Joey would leave for work. From the moment I arrived, Wendy was in tears. I had the responsibility of caring for my daughter and my granddaughter. I would sit with Wendy and ask her what she would like for breakfast. I would get moans in response; I would persist until she ate. Once I got her to eat breakfast, I would make her take a shower and get dressed. Her house was so dark and quiet. While she showered, I would open the blinds and windows. The house needed some sunlight and fresh air. I believe the darkness added to her depression; she was so isolated. I would make the beds, do the dishes and just try to straighten up the best that I could.

Wendy was usually still getting ready when Madison woke up. When Madison began to stir, my heart would jump, and I would run to her aid. It was like being a new mother all over again, and I loved it. I fed her and dressed her; it was magic. One day I put on the mobile in her bedroom that played "Imagine" by John Lennon as she sat in her crib. Out of nowhere, Wendy came running into the room crying, "Shut it off Mom! I cant listen to it!"

I didn't know how to turn it off, so I grabbed Madison, closed the door and went into the living room. Wendy was still crying, "I can't do this anymore, Mom. When am I going to get better? I can't listen to that song. It makes me too upset." I put Madison down in her bassinet; she was fine. Wendy needed me; I put my arms around her and hugged her, drying her tears, trying to calm her down. She was desperate and in so much pain that it broke my heart. Finally Wendy calmed down and finished getting dressed. We all needed to get out of the house.

Basically, that was how we spent the next few months, just like that day. I would go anywhere she wanted to go, buy her anything that she wanted, take her out to eat, but nothing seemed to bring a smile to her beautiful face. My life became a living hell too. I watched my daughter drag herself out of bed every day. It was an effort for her to get dressed or eat. The continuous gloom was very hard to bear.

On the other hand, I had my granddaughter, Madison. She was the greatest gift I could ever hope for. I watched her every move with such amazement and adoration. I was just so fascinated with everything she was. However, in a way, I was afraid to show Wendy how much I loved Madison. Wendy's thought process was a little off. I didn't want her to think Madison was more important to me than she was. I loved them both, one as a daughter, and one as a granddaughter.

After Wendy was introduced to Postpartum Resource Center and met Sonia, our whole family finally learned about postpartum depression. Joey and I went with Wendy to a "family night" meeting at the center. We both found it extremely educational. In addition, we also attended Wendy's appointments with her therapist and psychiatrist. It was definitely a group effort. We all wanted to see Wendy get better. This was not "our" Wendy, and we would do whatever it took to get her back.

Through a Mother's Eyes: Wendy's Mommy

In order for Wendy to get better, she needed plenty of rest, exercise, therapy and medication. She needed to take care of herself before she could take care of anyone else. So she needed my support to help care for Madison, and I was prepared for the task.

Eight years have passed since this horrible nightmare. It was a long bumpy road, but we made it through. Wendy is a magnificent mother. To my utter joy, Evangeline was born without incident. She is just as perfect as Madison, and I love them both more than words can describe. I was prepared for anything and was willing to be there for my family.

We volunteer at the Postpartum Resource Center together. Had it not been for Sonia Murdock together with the other medical professionals who helped my daughter, I don't know what the result of this story would've been. Wendy probably would not be here to share this story. I do know this: if you know anybody who is possibly suffering from this horrible illness, get them help as soon as possible. Tell them our story and try to find them resources that they need to get better.

My New & Improved Life

I am a completely different person. I am so much more confident and truly more appreciative of every blessing that I have, and I am truly blessed. My life is my family!

Madison is a beautiful, intelligent eight-year-old going into the third grade. She is so unique; she's not your typical little girl. She is extremely mature, well beyond her years. Was never really into princesses and cartoons, more like vampires, werewolves and superheroes. She is extremely funny and witty, with a great sense of humor. She is a wonderful and caring friend and absolutely adores her little sister. She is so creative; she loves to paint, draw, write poems, keep journals and has very recently started playing acoustic guitar. She loves horses and actually competes regularly. She's a great dancer (with rhythm that she didn't get from me) and loves to perform at her recitals.

She loves to read books about anything and everything she finds interesting.

Madison is a perfectionist and is extremely driven, almost to a fault, and that worries me. She has a lot obsessive-compulsive traits that I had as a child. She collects everything like I did and cannot throw anything away. She worries like me, too, and is afraid of losing those close to her. She has an enormous fear of car accidents and thunderstorms, which is kind of typical of a child, but she obsesses over it. For now, I try to ease her anxieties and help her through as much as possible. If and when it becomes a problem, I will address it, possibly seeking help from a professional and using cognitive therapy. But most of all, Maddy is happy, full of love and life, and I am so, so proud of her. I love her with everything I have.

Evangeline! Beautiful Evangeline. She is two going on sixteen. She is 100 percent personality. She is a constant performer and can make you laugh hysterically no matter what she does. From the second she came into this earth, she was entertaining. Her smile and constant energy, not to mention her obvious cuteness, light up a room.

I was extremely concerned that Evangeline wasn't healthy right after she was born; not only was she susceptible to everything being she was a newborn, but I was taking Zoloft throughout the pregnancy. I knew that it was proven to be an acceptable medication for pregnant/breastfeeding women, but it was in my nature to worry. Every checkup that Evangeline has had since birth has come back perfect; she has exceeded every milestone and is as strong as an ox. She amazes me with everything that she achieves. I marvel over the fact that she is only two years old and is able to do so many of the things she does. She loves to act out all of the movies she watches and recites the lines verbatim. She dances, sings and loves to make a total mess out of everything.

Madison and Evangeline are two completely different little girls in every way, with the exception of their looks. They love each other so much; it so endearing to watch them together. Madison is daddy's little girl 100 percent, but Evangeline is attached to my leg at all times. She is my little buddy, and I love every second of it. Both of my girls are a gift from God, and I love the both of them with every stitch of my being.

As for me, I have changed and grown so much in seven and a half years. My friend OCD is gone for the most part, but she comes back to visit every once and a while. When she does pay a visit, I know it is only temporary and she'll be going home soon. Nothing is too important, and I see the lighter side of every situation. I am an annoyingly happy person, and I know it. I don't care what anybody thinks of me. If it's not broken, then don't fix it. I still try not to kill any bugs, except for mosquitoes. I no longer do things over and over again until they are perfect, and I get ready in fifteen minutes as opposed to hours. I no longer collect and hoard things; now I collect and use them. I try to be extremely organized and clean, although my girls and all the dogs make it extremely difficult. My relationship with my family has never been better and I am so grateful. As far as the sperm donor; he is no longer a part of my life and I am very happy with that decision. My goal in life is to stay healthy and happy so that I can be there for my girls. I want to watch them grow and succeed in everything they do. They are my new "obsessions." My relationship with my husband has only gotten stronger. He is the true definition of a soul mate. Joey was sent to me from up above, and God has truly blessed me.

My Angels

*I*t has taken me about three and a half years to complete my story, and it is not as easy as I thought it would be. I figured it would be a walk in the park, writing a story about myself. Boy was I wrong. I had to rehash every horrible memory while trying to record that horrible time in my life. I cried a lot during this whole ordeal. Believe it or not, I am crying as I write this now. I have learned so many things about myself and life in eight years. I know now that I am a very strong person. I am also a more confident person; I can do anything if I put my mind to it. I am no longer afraid of everything. Being in fear all the time was a horrible way to live my life, and I know that now. I also know that I wouldn't change one thing in my life. If I didn't go through postpartum depression, then I wouldn't be where I am now. It was the worst possible thing that I have ever experienced, but it changed everything for me in so many ways that were for the best. It has been a long journey, and I have met so many wonderful people along the way. These people have made such a huge, positive impact on my life.

To Lori, my Lamaze instructor: if I never made my appointment to go for Lamaze class, I never would've met you. Running into you saved my life, and that's why you are my first angel. You brought me to angel number two, your sister and my therapist, Irene.

Irene, you are more than a therapist, you are a dear friend to me. I will always remember all that you did for my family and me. You took a terrified girl and molded her into a confident loving mother, not to mention that you helped and cured my OCD. You were with me all the way, and I love you for that. You saved my life! Everyone who knows and loves you is very lucky to have you. (Reader note: to this day, I still have a relationship with Irene as her patient and as her friend.)

Sonia, angel number three: once again I find myself in tears because I can't find the words to express how much you mean to me. What you did for my family and me is impossible to put a value on. Everything that you do every day for complete strangers is so selfless. You provide something extraordinary and extremely noble for women and their families, all of whom are in need. You have saved so many lives, including mine, with your humanity and compassion. You completely changed my life in so many ways that I am indebted to you always and will do whatever it takes to help your cause. Thank God for you!

That brings me to Dr. Abey, angel number four, who is my psychiatrist. You stuck with me and didn't give up. You are, also, more than a doctor: you are my friend. You were so persistent, yet caring; you made it your mission to help me get better. All that I needed was patience and time.

Ilene, angel number five: you were the voice with no face that helped me through my darkest hours. You inspired me to get better and gave me the courage to carry on. Hearing your story gave me hope that I would get better. You also inspired me to follow in your footsteps and do phone support so that I could provide the same help for someone else. Meeting you for the first time was such an honor.

These five women saved my life. Without their help and knowledge, I doubt I would still be here. My daughter wouldn't have a mother, and my husband would be a widower. Not to mention Evangeline, who would have never been born. Just thinking of that possibility is devastating. I got a second chance, and I am so appreciative. The moral to this story is: go to Lamaze class.

Sadly enough, depression is temporary and curable. I say this is sad because depression is such a gloomy, friendless, dark, horrible place, and a lot of people never get the help they need. Even worse is to go through depression as a new mother. I could not put into words the unbearable feeling of despair. It's like trying to describe a color to someone that they have never seen. It is virtually impossible.

Postpartum depression is real. It is not something that you can just kick, and it truly requires immediate medical attention. I wrote this story to help mothers and their families get through this dark and difficult time. If I can help just one person, then this is all worth it. The Postpartum Resource Center of New York is a non-profit, self-help organization. Your donations make this organization possible, so please help.

The Postpartum Resource Center of New York provides invaluable help and information to mothers, fathers, families, social service agencies and the medical community. However, we cannot continue to operate and grow our programs and services without your immediate financial support. Our goal is to further empower parents and the community to improve the lives of families by addressing issues involved with maternal/mental health and parenting with psychiatric disabilities.

What will happen if the Postpartum Resource Center of New York does not gain funding for essential services? What if the Postpartum Resource Center of New York does not continue to exist? The answer is that New York residents will no longer have an agency with respected experts whose sole purpose is getting women and families the help they need for prenatal and postpartum depression/anxiety and psychosis. New York will no longer have a dedicated agency that works to prevent tragedies such as those that have been highlighted in the media regarding mothers and babies.

It is critical that we have your support now so that our operations may continue now and for years to come. New York State moms, dads, their families and communities are counting on you to become a part of helping keep our valuable services available, so please join us now by becoming a supporter to save lives and build healthy families in your community. A copy of the Postpartum Resource Center of New York, Inc.'s latest financial statement may be requested from the New York State Department of Law Charities Bureau or from our office.

> NYS Department of Law
> Charities Bureau
> 120 Broadway - 3rd Floor
> New York, NY 10271
> (212) 416-8401
> http://www.charitiesnys.com

My Angels

Postpartum Resource Center of New York, Inc.
109 Udall Road
West Islip, NY 11795
(631) 422-2255.
www.postpartumny.org

Acknowledgments

To all of the friends and family members who were patient and stuck with me: I thank you so much for not judging me and for understanding. I love you all and am so fortunate to have all of you in my life.

Denise and Lauren: My "Blood Sisters", if is wasn't for Denise and Lauren pushing me to finish my book, giving me the confidence to continue and introducing me to Yvonne Kamerling and Janet Yudcwitz of Legwork Team Publishing, this book would never have gone to the printers. Thank you!

Stonch, you are my "bestest" friend. I love you so much, and I will never leave your side. That means you will never get rid of me no matter how hard you try. I see a "Woogie Stonches" in our future.

Ke-ke, you always did whatever you could for me and made me smile and laugh through it. Thank you for not giving up on me. I love you! "In the Bedroom" will always make me cry to the point of hysteria. By the way, "thank you for inviting me, I'm really having a good time!"

Bern, so many times I have wanted to strangle you, but whenever you are not around. I actually miss you. You are a great sister-in-law and an even better friend, no matter what Joe says. We have so many good times together, and whenever I am sad and need a good laugh, I know I can always count on you. It kills me to say this, but I love you. Be nice to the bumblebees.

My Liz and Triss! I feel like I have raised you both alongside your mother. You both grew up too fast, right before my eyes. I love you both so much, and you have no idea how much you helped me through such a rough time in my life.

Lilly, I want you to know that I love you, and I am so proud to have you as a sister-in-law. In the beginning, I was so distracted by my unhappy life that I didn't take the time to get to know you better. You have witnessed my highs and my lows and have always been there to support me. Watching you with Kyle and seeing how much you adore that beautiful boy makes me so proud to have you as my sister. My brother is so lucky to have you!

Nicole, you are me and Madison is you! Altogether we are awesome. I love you so much. You are the little sister I always wanted and finally got. I can talk to you about anything and nothing for hours. I would do anything for you, but I think you know that. You are such a caring, loving person, and I am so proud of you. Your heart is so big, and I admire that enormously.

Thom(ass), you were my first baby doll, and I had so much fun torturing you. I will never forget the Bahamas. You remind me so much of Grandpa that it warms my heart. You are probably one of the funniest people I know, and I love you so much.

Acknowledgments

Aunt Andrea, I don't even know how to describe how you fit into my life. You are my Godmother and my aunt, but you have always been there for me no matter what, and you never ever gave up on me. You are so special to me, and I love you so much. I knew how heartbroken you were for me when I was going through this whole ordeal. You tried everything you could to make it better for me. Thank you.

And I can't forget Uncle Tommy! You are one patient man, and have been right there with Aunt Andrea. You are a great father; and I love you too. I can't apologize enough for ruining your California trip with my "Sweet 16" temper tirade.

Grandma (Gramagra), the matriarch of our family: if it weren't for you, I definitely wouldn't be here. You were my playmate, and I was your doll. I know I am your *favorite*. I love you.

My brothers, Michael and Tommy: we are so alike and so different at the same time. Sometimes, hearing your voices or seeing your faces gave me the strength to go on. I couldn't imagine either of you explaining to anyone how and why your sister died. I love you both very much.

Michael, you were my partner in crime for the most important years of my life. You did whatever you could to protect me from getting hurt, even when I wouldn't listen. I will never forget that. There were so many times when you were my father more so than my brother and you took care of me. You helped so much in raising me with Mommy and Vito, and I thank you so much, big brother. My heart aches when I think of all the things we have gone through together,

Acknowledgments

many bad, but so many good. You are such an awesome father, and I am so proud of you. You have no idea.

Tommy, my baby brother; you are the male version of me. When you moved to Florida, you took a part of me with you; I was so heartbroken and devastated. Your mommy did such a good job raising you because you are such an extraordinary person. You have so much love to give and are so selfless; I absolutely adore you. Even though you are so far away, I feel like you're with me always.

Vito, a.k.a. J-man, Shaft, Papa Veet, P-pa and Grandpa. You are my father, even though you don't want to take credit for it. You gave Mommy, Michael and me a wonderful life. I have no idea where I would be in life if it wasn't for you. You gave us stability and were always there. You loved us always and gave us support the only way you knew how: through laughter, and I have not stopped laughing yet. I love you so much Dad! Thank you for being you and never changing. I wouldn't want it any other way.

My mother, Patricia: I love you, "Always." I know that you had your doubts about your own mothering skills. You felt so much guilt because you didn't feel that you were a good enough mother to Michael and me when we younger, but you were. You molded us into the adults that we are today, and I am pretty outstanding, if I do say so myself. You have been my number one fan and biggest supporter in everything I have done so far in my life. You have helped me up every time I have fallen. You rose above all the nonsense in your life and came out on top, and you are my role model. You're not only my mother, you are my best friend, too. You are the world's best mother and grandmother. I couldn't go a day without talking to you; I need you. Anyway, I am just like you, so I have to be a good mother, too. I love you more than words can say. You are the wind beneath my wings! *Always* . . .

To my husband Joey: you are my life and my love. I don't know what I did in this life to get you as my husband, but it must have been something very good. I am so lucky, and I know it. You are such a wonderful father. I only wish that I could've had a father like you. Our girls are truly blessed. Just watching you with Madison and Evangeline makes my heart melt. I know how much you love me, and I see it in everything that you do for me. I fall in love with you more and more, each and every day. You gave me the strength to carry on and you love me unconditionally, not to mention how extremely handsome you are!

To my beautiful daughters, Madison and Evangeline: you are my life and the sole reason that I carried on. I did all of this for you. Watching the both of you grow is my greatest joy in life. I live to see your beautiful faces and hear your laughter. You both are my heart and my soul, and I love you more than anything on this earth. My jelly beans!

All day, every day!

Resources

ORGANIZATIONS

National Suicide Prevention Lifeline
If you are planning or fear that you may harm yourself, your baby or others, you need to call your healthcare provider, dial 911 (emergency services) or go to the nearest hospital emergency room. Help is available.

Available 24 hours a day:
Call 1-800-273-TALK
1-800-273-8255
www.suicidepreventionlifeline.org

Baby Safe Haven: Do Not Abandon Your Newborn
If you are pregnant and afraid to tell anyone, or if you do not know what to do with your newborn baby, call for help or take the baby to any hospital emergency room. Your secret and your baby will be safe. The police will not be called. You will not have to answer any questions. Confidential help and support are available for you.

AMT Children of Hope Safe Haven Program
Call 1-877-796-HOPE

Resources

1-877-796-4673
www.amtchildrenofhope.com

Child Abuse Prevention
Childhelp USA National Child Abuse Hotline
Call 1-800-4-A-CHILD
1-800-422-2253
www.childhelp.org

Postpartum Support International
Dedicated to helping women and families suffering from perinatal mood and anxiety disorders. World-wide resource network of volunteer coordinators, Chat with the Experts, annual international conference, membership with quarterly newsletter.
copyright, 2010 Postpartum Support International

For help contact:
Helpline: 1-800-944-4PPD
1-800-944-4773
www.postpartum.net

Postpartum Resource Center of New York
Finding the help you need!
Free and confidential emotional support and self help education with Moms on Call and Family Support Telephone Volunteers, State-wide on-line Perinatal Mood Disorders Resource Directory, Postpartum Resource Center of New York's Training Institute including the Postpartum Resource Center of New York's Circle of Caring Pregnancy and Postpartum Depression Support Group, Volunteer Network and Advocacy Helpline:

Resources

631-422-2255

www.postpartumny.org

Health Resources and Service Administration (HRSA)

The Marce Society

www.marcesociety.com

MedEdPPD

www.mededppd.org

Online PPD Support Group

www.ppdsupportpage.com

Postpartum Progress Blog

Founded by Katherine Stone

www.postpartumprogress.com

Melanie's Battle

Website and information about Melanie Blocker Stokes and postpartum psychosis

www.melaniesbattle.org

Jenny's Light

For national awareness of all perinatal mood disorders including postpartum depression

www.jennyslight.org

International OCD Foundation

617-973-5801

Resources

www.ocfoundation.org

OCD Tribe

www.ocdtribe.com

PUBLICATIONS

Dropping the Baby and Other Scary Thoughts:
Breaking the Cycle of Unwanted Thoughts in Motherhood

Karen Kleinman, MSW

Amy Wenzel

Therapy and the Postpartum Woman:
Notes on Healing Postpartum Depression for Clinicians and
the Women Who Seek their Help

Karen Kleinman, MSW

What Am I Thinking?
Having a Baby After Postpartum Depression

Karen Kleinman. MSW

The Postpartum Husband
Practical Solutions for Living with Postpartum Depression

Karen Kleinman, MSW

This Isn't What I Expected
Overcoming Postpartum Depression

Karen Kleinman, MSW

Valarie Raskin, MD

About the Author

Wendy Isnardi lives in Suffolk County, New York, along with her husband and two young daughters. Since the birth of her first daughter, she has been a staunch supporter and volunteer for the Postpartum Resource Center of New York. This is a non-profit agency dedicated to helping women and their families survive their ordeals with depression during pregnancy and depression following the birth of their children. She has dedicated countless time and energy to assure that the center continues to exist and provide the support that women need in order to beat serious mental diseases. She has put fighting women's depression on the forefront of her life with great personal sacrifice.

Nobody Told Me

For more information regarding Wendy Isnardi and her work,
visit her Website: www.nobodytoldmebook.com.

Additional copies of this book may be purchased online from
LegworkTeam.com; Amazon.com; BarnesandNoble.com;
or via the author's Website: www.nobodytoldmebook.com.

You can also obtain a copy of the book by visiting
L.I. Books Bookstore
80 Davids Drive, Suite One
Hauppauge, NY 11788
or by ordering it from your favorite bookstore.